# LESSONS FROM A ROAD WARRIOR

# LESSONS FROM A
# ROAD WARRIOR

How I fell off a horse, earned 15 million air miles, got
sand in my shoes and learned how to invest

by

## DR. JOHN RUTLEDGE

Edited by Elizabeth S. Rutledge

Published by Rutledge Research

Copyright © 2008 Rutledge Research
www.rutledgeresearch.com
www.rutledgecapital.com

Cover design, illustrations and interior layout
design by Elizabeth S. Rutledge

Printed in the United States of America

ISBN 978-0-9818381-0-6

# Table of Contents

# Table of Figures

LESSONS FROM A ROAD WARRIOR

# Preface

Writing this book has been a very good experience for me. In reviewing my intellectual journey, I was able to revisit all of the family, friends and mentors I have learned from in my life. What a generous and extraordinary group of people! You will get to know many of them—Mom, Dad, Tom, Jessica, Manda, John, Katie, Elizabeth, Grandma Flora, Uncle Bill, Nurse Evans, Jerry, Bake, Chris, Deborah, Pamela, Larry, Charlie, Jack, Joe, Nick, Art, Bob and many others—as you read through the book. Some have Nobel prizes; some have eighth-grade educations. All have great wisdom and strong character. This book contains the lessons I learned from all of them.

Thanks to them, I have the coolest job in the world. I live in the freest, richest country on the planet. I get to go anywhere I want around the globe, any time I want, to explore the things that make me curious. I get to talk with the most interesting people alive about strange and wonderful ideas. I get to meddle in the policies of nations, the strategies of companies large and small, and in the allocation of massive portfolios. I get to invest large amounts of money in public and private equities. I get to talk to millions of people on TV every week about the things I care about. I don't have to wear a tie. I don't have to lift anything heavy. And some days I get to walk on the beach.

This is really cool.

- JR

# 1

## Introduction

I grew up in the 1950s in Winthrop Harbor, Illinois, a town of 1,500 people on the shore of Lake Michigan. The people there were half farmers and half factory workers; so I learned to grow things, I learned to make things, and I learned to respect people who did both. Although there were many churches in Winthrop Harbor, our principal religion was work.

As kids, our main occupations were pretending to do our homework, pretending to do our chores, and chasing whatever ball was appropriate to the season around an empty field. In the summer, we would sneak down to the lake and turn blue swimming in the 55-degree water, trying—and failing—to catch fish. In winter, we would sneak down to the swamp with a snow shovel and a broom to ice skate. The only time we ever left town was on Saturday mornings when we drove to Zion, the nearest metropolis, to shop for groceries. Zion was huge; they had 14,000 people there!

## Chekhov's Law

In order to learn anything, you have to get off the porch. I remember standing at the edge of the lake one summer day, squinting my 20/400 vision eyes and trying in vain to see Michigan, which my dad had told me was on the other side of the lake 80 miles away. I thought to

*Anton Chekhov*

myself, "Someday I'm going to go over there and see Michigan for myself."

Years later, I call this idea Chekhov's Law; it's how I learn everything. In one of Anton Chekhov's more than 200 wonderful short stories—I forget which one—a character says, "If you want to understand Bulgarians, you have to go to Bulgaria. You can't just read about them in the newspapers." I have been "going to Bulgaria" since my 16th birthday, when I hitchhiked to California without telling my poor parents that I was leaving.

After 43 years and roughly 15 million air miles, I am sure that Chekhov was right. The only way to get to know people you are curious about is to go to their country, keep your eyes open and your mouth shut, have dinner at their houses and get to know their kids.

When you follow Chekhov's Law, you learn that the differences among people are not as important as the similarities. That's especially important today because people all over the world can see each other in real-time on their TV screens. We all have a tendency to blame far-away people—the ones in other "tribes"—when things don't go well in our own lives. The end result is escalating conflict around the world.

I'll talk more about this subject in Chapter 9 when I discuss what recent advances in brain science can show us about economics, politics and conflict.

## Saper Vedere

The second most important thing I've ever learned is how to see. Not with your eyes, lucky for me—with your brain.

Leonardo da Vinci is certainly the most creative man the Western world has ever produced. (I say Western world because he has rivals in both the Middle East and Asia.) Leonardo's contemporaries asked him to reveal the secret of his genius that allowed him to draw, paint, sculpt and invent new

*Leonardo da Vinci* [1]

technologies. He replied, "saper vedere," Tuscan for the English phrase "to know how to see."[2] It is not the skill with a paintbrush or chisel or the details of a design that makes a masterpiece, he believed, but the ability to develop a picture in your head of what you want to create before you begin the work.

My objective in writing this book is to help you to *know how to see* the global economy and financial markets by understanding the links between government policy, capital formation and growth, as well as the fundamental forces that drive change. Then I will discuss how to use this framework to understand the value of businesses so you can build and manage a successful investment portfolio.

---

[1] I made this sketch of Leonardo's *Self Portrait*, which hangs in the Royal Library in Turin, sitting in my favorite seat (1C) on a flight from New York to Seattle late one night. I was following Leonardo's advice, doing several things at once to exercise my brain—drawing with a pencil in my left hand, writing notes (backwards, from right to left, as Leonardo did in his notebooks), and listening to Chinese lessons on my earphones. In the next seat, my neighbor, Dr. Ruth, woke up from a nap and said, "This is most interesting."

[2] S. Bramly, *Leonardo: the Artist and the Man*, (1995). This book is full of wonderful stories about Leonardo's life. My favorite is Leonardo's 1502-1503 period when he served as architect and military engineer for Cesare Borgia, who was the illegitimate son of Pope Alexander VI, the Duke of Romagna and the inspiration for Niccolo Machiavelli's masterpiece, *The Prince* (1515). In the fall of 1502 and early months of 1503, Cesare Borgia, his sister Lucrezia, Leonardo, Machiavelli, and Luca Pacioli—Leonardo's friend, mathematician, and author of the first written treatise on double-entry bookkeeping—lived together in the same house! I would pay anything to be at those dinners.

But first, I will take you on a tour of some of the lessons I learned along the way.

## It's Okay to Fail

When I give lectures at universities around the world, I always save time after the lecture to meet the students and answer their questions. They always ask the same things: where should they go to business school, what should they study, where should they work for their first job and what do they have to do to be successful?

I always give them the same answer. It's not *what you do* that matters; it's *what you are.* The world is full of smart, ambitious young people who know how to do all sorts of things. But people you can count on all the time are very scarce. You can teach skills, but you can't teach character.

One of the best ways to develop strong character is to try and fail. I believe that bruises—not books—are the best teachers, and that calluses—not advanced degrees—are the real evidence of higher learning. In America today, we use too much energy celebrating our victories and not enough energy learning from our failures.

If you want to be successful, do something you love, learn something new every day, find the smartest, most decent people you can and stay as close to them as possible so you can learn how they think. Be someone other people can count on, and don't be afraid to take risks—don't be afraid to fail. In my career, I learned the most from my mistakes—I wouldn't trade them for anything in the world.

Growing up, my family heroes were Grandpa Brock, who walked nine miles every morning to his job at the asbestos factory in the next town; Grandma Flora, who survived the Oklahoma Dust Bowl and built a barn with her own hands when she was 60 years old; and Uncle John, who rode the railcars during the Great Depression looking for work. But my biggest hero was my dad, who fought in two wars in the engine room of a destroyer escort, and then worked for a dozen companies in the 1950s before he found steady work. Dad went to work every day before dawn. He was the guy everyone in town came to for help when things went wrong.

I learned to ride a horse by falling off—repeatedly. My Grandpa Elijah taught me that it was not a sin to be thrown from a horse, but it *was* a sin to stay on the ground. And it was an even bigger sin to be too afraid to try in the first place.

*Me Riding Baldy in 1958*

Most of what I know has come from the bumps and bruises I got while trying to do things I didn't know how to do. That may be why I have worked for myself and owned my own business for the past 35 years. With my resume, I'm the only one willing to hire me.

Showing up counts too. Woody Allen is supposed to have said that in life, showing up is 80%. Nurse Evans, the crusty old nurse at Spring Bluff grade school, would have busted Woody's chops. Nurse Evans handed out band-aids and made us take our eye exams,[3] but her real job was to make sure we showed up every morning. I learned how to show up one cold winter school morning when I was in third grade. I had succeeded in talking my dad into letting me stay home, based on one imagined ailment or another, and was just settling into a heaping bowl of corn flakes when I heard a knock at the kitchen door. It was Nurse Evans driving a herd of a dozen or so of my fellow malingerers, dressed

---

[3] My greatest achievement in grade school was to avoid getting glasses until I was in the fifth grade. (Glasses were not cool in the 1950s.) That meant fooling Nurse Evans every year—a formidable challenge. I did it by memorizing which way all the little E's were pointing on the eye chart as I walked past it—slowly—on my way into her office. In fifth grade I got busted.

in boots, mittens and snow pants, back to school. I pulled on my snow pants like all the rest. It was the last time I came down with a mysterious illness.

I also learned about being careful. When I was sixteen years old, I had a summer job as a helper on a Pepsi truck. One day, I was sitting in the helper's (shotgun) seat of a huge Pepsi truck, waiting to go. I was looking very cool in my Pepsi work shirt—chicks dig Pepsi shirts—peering out the side window at the large rectangular rearview mirror on the right side of the truck. The driver gunned the engine to try to make a left-hand turn onto a four-lane highway before the light turned red. As we turned the corner, a wall of Pepsi, nearly 500 cases in all, blotted out the sun in my rearview mirror. The complete contents of one side of the truck were catapulted onto the four-lane highway. The driver's helper—that would be me—had forgotten to close the side doors and secure the load at our last stop.

For two hours, I picked up broken Pepsi bottles with a broom and a piece of cardboard while the driver, who was personally responsible for the value of the load, repeatedly clenched and unclenched his fists by the side of the road. This ended my short but colorful career at Pepsi. I learned two things that day: 1) I was not cut out for jobs that required me to pay attention; and 2) Don't mess with the laws of nature.

But I soon ignored the lesson. I needed a new amplifier for my guitar—being in a rock and roll band was the only sure way to get girls—so I decided to get another job, this time as a short-order cook in a drive-in restaurant. No problem, the boss said. When the carhops brought in a new order, they clipped it onto a revolving wheel so I could turn it around and read the order. I failed to tell him that I was so nearsighted (20/400) that I couldn't see the wheel at all, much less the orders. By the end of the first night, I was washing root beer mugs, my exclusive assignment, while the boss cooked all the food himself. There was no second night. The morals here: 1) Don't sign up for something unless you can deliver it, and 2) Vanity can be very expensive.

Halfway through high school I thought, "This is boring, I'm going to go to college. Now." Surprisingly, I was admitted and entered college as a 16 year-old, where I immediately joined a fraternity (fraternities were cool). During my first year, I applied myself with diligence to the most important subjects: playing pool, learning to drink bourbon without making a face, and (at least thinking about) how to get girls. I did less well in attending class and other academic areas. After an undistinguished freshman year, the dean and I agreed I should go and find myself— somewhere else—until I learned how to deliver on commitments.

That brings me to my next career, this time as a (pretend) scientist. I got a job at a paint factory as a quality-control technician. I only earned $62 per week but I got to wear a white lab coat (not as good as a Pepsi shirt but still very cool). My job was testing every batch of paint for color, hardness and viscosity by measuring how long it took for paint to dribble out of a little cup with a hole in the bottom. Well, *almost* every batch. It seems I neglected to test a 1,500-gallon vat one day, which an industrial customer later used to paint an entire factory. When the paint dried, it literally fell off the walls—apparently the entire batch had been mixed without any resin, the stuff that makes paint stick. My boss and I decided that it was time to for me go back to school. Immediately.

Armed with recent evidence that I was not well-suited to earn a living in the real world, I decided to become a college professor. This time I applied myself with a vengeance, even copying textbooks by hand to memorize them. I studied. I showed up. I turned in term papers on time. This work helped me earn my bachelor's degree and a place in graduate school, where I completed my economics Ph.D. in less than three years. I had finally learned the work habits that I have used ever since to build my career as an economist, investor, and business and investment advisor. Each step along the way helped me learn how to work, how to handle myself, and how to be a good team member.

I needed these lessons to handle a very difficult experience I had in the mid-'80s. My partner Deborah Allen and I had raised $2 million in venture capital to build a unique family of mutual funds, in which we allocated shareholder funds among a group of first-rate institutional money managers. After two years in business, we had succeeded in growing the fund to $70 million and were within sight of the $100 million total asset level we needed to break even as a management company, i.e., the point where we would be able to stop burning through our capital to support current operating expenses. But the 500-point drop in the stock market on October 19, 1987, changed all of our plans.

Our funds had performed very well during the crash—we were among the top-performing funds in the country that day—but investors lost their appetite for the market. It became very difficult to grow the assets of the fund. With our break-even point looking unreachable, we examined our alternatives. We could raise more capital and risk losing even more of our investors' money. We could sell out to a larger fund, which didn't seem right, since investors had come to our fund specifically to invest with us. Or we could simply close the fund down and send our shareholders their money back, and our venture capital investors what was left of theirs. We chose the latter course and wound down operations.

Looking back, I think we threw in the towel too early. If we had had the tenacity to hunker down a little longer, and faith that the market would rebound, we would have made it. But I learned some valuable lessons. I learned the value of a good partner when things are not going well. I learned how to lose money in the market without losing faith in the future. And I learned not to start a venture without sufficient capital to see it through to completion.

These lessons and hundreds more like them, along with the friends and partners I learned them from, are the most valuable assets I own. Falling off a horse—and getting back on again—is the only way I know how to learn them.

## Lessons from Grandpa Brock

Grandpa Brock was a sort of Calvinist Optimist, a person who believes that life is hard but that hard times are good for you because they make you strong.

It's not difficult to figure out where Grandpa got this idea. He grew up in the last decade of the 19th century in the middle of coal-mining country in Turtle Town, Tennessee. (Turtle Town is a suburb of Duck Town. I'm not making this up.) Then, as a young man, he moved to the Midwest to seek his fortune in the booming industrial sector. He never found his fortune but he did find work—50 years in a Johns Manville asbestos factory without missing a day. He lived to be 96 years old. I never heard him complain.

Grandpa Brock gave me my first great investment deal. His favorite entertainment was sitting in his recliner and listening to Jack Brickhouse on the radio, calling the plays while the Chicago Cubs lost another game. While doing so, he invariably chewed tobacco. Once every week, he sent me with a dime to Charlie's Market, two blocks away, to buy a new block of Spark Plug chewing tobacco (which he knew cost only a nickel). When I returned with the prize, he always told me that I could keep the nickel if I promised to save it. Done deal!

That may still be the best investment I have ever made. Revenue, a nickel. Cost Of Goods Sold, zero. Gross Profit, a nickel. Sales, General, and Administrative expenses, zero. Operating Profit, a nickel. Taxes, zero. Profit After Tax, a nickel. Capital, zero. Return on Invested Capital, infinite. Not bad for a 10 year-old.

Grandpa Brock's philosophy can be boiled down to four simple rules:

1. Show up

2. Work hard

3. Take care of your tools

4. Save your money

Not too elegant, perhaps, but still the best advice I have ever heard. Works for a person, for a family, for a business, or for a nation. Grandpa Brock's rules are great for today's economy, where growth is slowing, prices are going up, and global competition is fierce. Write them down.

The things I learned from Grandpa Brock not only made me a better worker, a better manager and a better business owner; they also made me a better investor. I learned to identify corporate waste and low-return capital, and I learned the value of managers who are not afraid to make the tough changes necessary to make their companies successful.

## The Value of Pruning

The hard lessons are the ones you never forget, like the summer I learned that pruning early and pruning often is a good idea. My cousin Bob and I were looking for a way to make some money one summer when we got the idea to raise a vegetable garden, and then sell our harvest door-to-door in the neighborhood. Uncle Bill let us use an empty field behind his chicken coop and God was willing to provide the sunshine—all we had to do was buy the seed and do a little work. We figured there was a good chance we'd get rich and retire before we started high school.

When we showed up the first day with our corn, tomato, pepper, onion, cucumber and melon seeds, Uncle Bill showed us what to do. First you have to plow the field to prepare the ground for planting. "Then, when you plant the corn," he said, "make sure that you put two or three seeds in each hole. Later, when they sprout, and you see which one looks like the strongest plant, you pull the other little plants up by their roots and throw them out."

Bob and I listened, looked at each other and nodded our heads—we had been taught to show respect for our elders—but we could see right then that the old man was a fool. We could get three times more corn from three stalks of corn than we could from one. Why throw them out? So when the soft, green sprouts appeared a few weeks later, we watered them all and let nature take its course. Before the summer was out, we had a beautiful field of ripe, sweet corn. The only problem was that the stalks of corn, which were supposed to be "knee high by the Fourth of July," were only fourteen inches tall on Labor Day. And the ears of corn, while plentiful and perfectly formed, were approximately the size of a Q-tip. (Now I know where they get those tiny ears of corn that always show up on buffet tables.)

Bob and I didn't get rich that summer. We canned the entire crop—147 ears—in an ordinary pickle jar, which I still keep on my mantle so that I never forget Uncle Bill's lesson about pruning. When you allow too many projects to compete for the same resources, none of them are likely to turn out well.

Pruning is just as powerful in the corner office or on the trading floor as it was behind the chicken coop. My friend Peter Drucker wrote in *The Effective Executive* that it is often more important for a manager to decide what *not* to do—to break the momentum of last year's activities—than to make plans about what to do. He advised managers to stop doing 25% of the things they did last year in order to ensure that they will have the uncommitted resources to pursue their next great idea. Peter was a very wise man.

In asset management and value creation, the discipline of pruning is everything. Growing companies pick up assets like gym socks pick up cockleburs. Growing sales mean more people, desks, telephones and typewriters. Growth also means more inventory, receivables, machines, and factories. All this takes money—usually other people's money—which bloats a company's balance sheet and drags down its return on capital and its value to investors.

The same is true when managing portfolios. Many investors spend all their energy looking for good companies to buy, but pay no attention to them once they are in the portfolio. It is important to review a portfolio regularly—pruning shears in hand—to remove the companies whose fundamentals no longer make them attractive to own, and to trim small positions that distract your energy.

## Bake's Principles

Of all the stories I ever wrote, the one that generated the most mail from readers was the story of my first business partner, V. P. Baker. Bake—as he liked to be called—taught me that the owner's intangible capital can be more important to a business than its physical assets. It's true in the investment business too—your reputation is your most valuable asset.

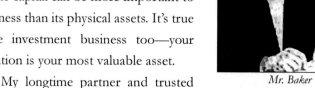

*Mr. Baker*

My longtime partner and trusted friend Jerry St. Dennis and I first met Bake in 1978. Bake was already 89 years old—I was 30. Bake's colorful career included being a WWI fighter pilot, a borax prospector, a mule dentist, a wildcat oilman, an orange rancher, and a real estate developer. He was a wonderfully principled man. I keep a portrait of him in my office to remind me of his advice.

Here are eight business principles that Jerry and I learned from Bake. They may help you.

1.  Do the right thing. A handshake with a person who always tries to do the right thing is more comforting than a bushel of legal documents signed by a bad guy.

2.  Don't hide the ball. When you lose a big account or when you discover an error in your financials, don't hide it from your banker or your employees. Tell them what happened. That way they can share the burden of fixing the problem. At first they will be surprised when you do this—people are used to hearing lies—but over time they will learn to trust your word. Besides, as Bake put it, "If you have to make money by tricking people, you are not much of a businessman."

3.  You don't need to shout and swear to make your point. If others do so, walk out of the room. You don't have to do business with jerks.

4.  Leave something on the table for the other guy. The best business deal isn't the one that maximizes your advantage or your profits. It is the one that maximizes the chance that the next time you run into the other person you will both be glad to see each other.

5.  Make everyone your customer. If, as Peter Drucker wrote, the purpose of a business is to create a customer—someone who chooses to do business with you over and over—then it is important for your customer to enjoy the experience every time. Treat your customers in a way that will make them want to come back.

6.  Stick to your principles. Hire people who are willing to live by them, teach them thoroughly and insist on total commitment. There's no room for diversity of principles in an organization.

7.  Make your principles tangible. I am no fan of executive retreats and the like, but sometimes they can be good opportunities to teach business principles. I make do with the portrait of Bake in my office to remind me that he is still watching. "What would Bake do?" is my standard way of approaching a problem.

8.  Principles are not for sale. Be prepared to walk away from a deal, any deal, rather than violate your principles to win it.

The twist, of course, is that businesses organized around principles are often more successful and make more money than those organized around the idea that greed is good. Nice guys often finish first.

Bake's principles are especially important when you're investing other people's money. Many people have the misunderstanding that investing is a game of sharp elbows, tricky deals and inside information. They think that somewhere, there is a guy who has all the secrets. They are wrong. The secret to investing is hard work and sticking to your principles.

Now that I've told you about some of my guiding principles, I want to take you on a journey of the ideas that make up the way I think about economics and investing today. If you suffer from attention deficit disorder and would just like to eat the soup, rather than learn the recipe, you can read the short version contained in Chapter 2. If you are curious about ideas and want to know where they came from, or you just want to understand the ideas well enough to explain them to someone else, I invite you to read the entire book.

# 2

# Economics and Investing

T he most important thing to know about economics and investing is that you have to know the first one in order to do the second one well. In 1989, Deborah Allen and I wrote *Rust to Riches* to make the case that the demise of the U.S. economy had been overstated, and that the U.S. was *not* going to be taken over by Japan Inc. as many people then believed. After a decade of restructuring their businesses for low inflation, American companies were strong and lean. Japan was headed into a deflation, which would sap their economic strength. Those who undersold American companies would pay the price.

We told business managers that the lesson of the 1980s was that they should not be so focused on the day-to-day operations inside their businesses that they forget to manage the outside of their businesses— by making sure that their companies were structured to take advantage of the massive economic changes taking place in the global economy. The same goes for investors managing public or private equity portfolios.

Changes in government policies and in technology can lead to changes in behavior that turn normal markets on their heads.

This chapter is a short summary of the most important things I have learned about economic change—and how to use them to manage a portfolio.

## Growth is Good

Thirty-five years of traveling the world have convinced me that growth is the answer. Economic growth is the only reliable engine for lifting people out of poverty and improving their lives, and for providing challenging opportunities to engage young people's energies.

There are people who do not like growth. Some because they think it causes inflation. Some because they think it causes global warming. They are idiots. Growth is the greatest thing that ever happened.

Growth requires capital. Access to capital, along with people's focused productive energies, are the principal drivers of growth.

Capital comes in many forms: efficient factories, modern equipment, new technologies, high-speed communications networks, financial capital and a highly educated workforce, to name a few. All represent the stored energy of previous generations of investors, innovators, entrepreneurs, managers and workers. All make workers more productive, increase output, and provide paychecks that give people the resources to achieve their economic, personal and social goals. Incentives for creating capital and for the productive use of all forms of energy are the keys to increased growth.

As a young economist, I taught graduate and undergraduate students in macroeconomics, monetary theory, econometrics, international trade and finance. Like other academics, I taught students how to build and manipulate all the textbook models of economic behavior. I did so for three reasons. First, the models were precise and mathematically elegant, which made them both beautiful and easy to teach. Second, publishing journal articles about the models was the key to attaining the Holy Grail of the economics profession—tenure. And third, and most importantly, having never set foot in the real world, it was all I knew how to do.

Later I ventured into the real world, where I learned that the models were not up to the task of helping policy makers, business managers and investors understand change. Keeping my healthy respect for the limitations of economic models, my colleagues and I at Claremont Economics Institute (CEI) and later at Rutledge Capital developed a framework of our own to guide our thinking. That framework, of course, is a permanent work in progress. It underlies all of our work.

## Stuff Matters

The first pillar of our thinking framework is also the simplest: Stuff Matters. No macroeconomic analysis is complete without accounting for people's multi-trillion dollar holdings of "Stuff." What I mean by stuff is the collection of items on our balance sheets, including tangible assets (land, office buildings, collectibles, used cars and other physical claims on future services), financial assets (stocks, bonds, bank accounts, cash and all other claims on future cash flow), and all forms of liabilities (credit card debt, mortgages, and the obligation to service and repay the national debt).

Analyzing the income statement, i.e., GDP and its components, is just not possible without accounting for all the stuff on the balance sheets. That's true simply because there is so much stuff out there. This year, in 2008, U.S. GDP will amount to just over $14 trillion—this means that Americans will produce just over $14 trillion worth of goods and services with their current work. But this number is nothing in comparison with asset markets. At the end of 2007, even after a credit crunch and a year of falling home prices, Americans owned nearly $200 trillion worth of assets at market values—roughly 14 years worth of GDP. And that does not include the value of their human capital (another $200 tril-lion) or the value of the more than 700 million acres of land (another $10 trillion or so) owned by the federal government. In all, the U.S. bal-ance sheet likely amounts to more than 30 years worth of GDP.

Stuff matters too because the values of the individual items on our balance sheets determine our net worth and our solvency; they serve as collateral for our obligations and they influence our behavior. Asset values are set in markets based on investors' perceptions of the relative risks and after-tax returns of different assets and liabilities.

Assets are the key to understanding how policy works. Govern-ment policies that force abrupt changes in relative risks and returns of different assets and liabilities induce massive responses in desired hold-ings of private investors. They produce tsunamis of economic and finan-cial change that can swamp the effects described in textbooks.

## Shift Happens

Government economic policies influence our lives in many ways. Government taxes influence our paychecks, the prices of the things we spend them on, and our incentives to work, save and invest. Their big-gest and most convulsive impacts on the economy, however, occur when government policies drive a wedge between the returns on some assets relative to others, or when they temporarily disrupt the flow of informa-tion transmitted by asset prices. These balance sheet effects dominate all other events in driving economic change.

In the late 1970s, for example, rising inflation artificially enhanced the returns on tangible assets, like real estate, while rising income tax rates artificially depressed the after-tax returns on financial assets. The resulting shift of investor demands drove a boom in hard asset prices and destroyed three-quarters of the real value of the stock and bond markets.

As a second example, the 1981 Reagan policies of falling inflation and falling tax rates reversed this shift by boosting financial asset returns relative to returns on tangible assets. This led to a decade of restructuring in U.S. industry, rising investment spending and a 20-year bull market in bonds and stocks.

As a third example, the 1996 Telecom Act artificially subsidized the returns of communications companies that did business by using other companies' capital, known as Competitive Local Exchange Carriers or CLECs—at the expense of the companies that provided the capital to build the networks. The resulting wedge between their respective returns on capital led to massive overinvestment in the former, a multi-trillion dollar loss of market value for the latter, and contributed to both the stock market bubble of the late 1990s and the dot-com bust that followed.

The 2003 dividend tax cut provides a fourth example. The reduction in dividend tax rates from ordinary income levels to 15% abruptly raised the after-tax return on assets paying taxable dividends relative to the after-tax returns on all other assets. This return gap caused investors to shift their portfolios toward dividend-paying assets, which drove a huge increase in stock prices and subsequently led to a wave of changes in corporate dividend policies, such as the special dividend announced by Microsoft later that year.

Shift happens internationally too. The systematic opening of China to foreign investors has exposed the gap between the high Chinese returns on capital and returns in the U.S. and Europe, leading to a massive flow of capital out of Japan, the EU and the U.S. into China, which has fueled an extended period of high Chinese growth. The high returns earned on this capital have also increased the profits of U.S.-based companies as a share of sales by more than half; today more than half the profits of the companies in the S&P 500 are earned on sales outside the United States.

I will talk more about the economics of the balance sheet in Chapter 3.

## Thermo-Economics

The principal of arbitrage lies at the heart of all economic analysis. Indeed, the statement that people engage in arbitrage may be the only positive statement that economics has to make. Arbitrage, however, is immensely powerful, and in turn is simply a restatement of the bedrock of physics: the second law of thermodynamics.

Thermodynamics says that temperature differentials cannot persist over time between objects in physical communication, i.e., within the same closed system. In physics, when two objects are brought into contact, heat flows from the hotter to the colder object as long as there remains a temperature differential. This is known as the second law of thermodynamics—the most inviolable rule in all of science. At the final point where temperatures are equal, after which point there is no further tendency for temperature to change, the system is said to be in thermal equilibrium. Physicists call it *heat death*.

All activity in life is driven by the second law of thermodynamics. It is why the chemical reactions occur in our cells. It is why sunlight leads to photosynthesis. It is why volcanoes erupt and tectonic plates shift to make earthquakes. Thermodynamics explains why temperature and pressure differentials produce weather systems that cause storms. And it explains economics, where price, wage, or return differentials lead to the arbitrage behavior that drives prices and returns together and changes the allocation of resources.

Our "Shift Happens" methodology, discussed in the previous section, is nothing more than a restatement of the second law of thermodynamics in the language of economics and finance. Unfortunately, economists insist on analyzing what happens at the point of equilibrium. Thermodynamics, however, reminds us that nothing of interest happens at equilibrium. All change takes place *away* from equilibrium.

Thermodynamics deals with systems, not with particles. There is no thermodynamics of a particle. Recent work in far-from-equilibrium physics has led to a fuller understanding of the situations in which systems fail to adjust smoothly. These situations lead to system failures (blackouts), which help us understand recessions, depressions, currency collapses, credit-market failures and other discontinuous events in economics. Interestingly, Irving Fisher, Knut Wicksell and John Maynard Keynes studied these topics a century ago. I will discuss the implications of thermodynamics for economics and investing in Chapter 6.

## Asset Allocation

Most investors spend the lion's share of their time and energy on deciding which stock or bond to hold in their portfolios. In my experience, asset allocation is much more important: how to divide a portfolio among different markets and types of securities. If you get the asset allocation right, everything else will work out. If you get it wrong, you are sunk.

Professionals pay a lot of attention to asset allocation, but individual investors often overlook it. Too bad—today, investors can implement asset allocation decisions cheaply and easily. Exchange traded funds (ETFs), which aim to reproduce the average results of investing in different countries or different sectors, allow investors and investment advisors to manage asset allocation themselves, without high fees and without high turnover. Exchange traded funds are tailor-made for placing modest bets on the economic and financial storm systems I discussed above. I use them to do so myself.

Don't look to asset allocation for entertainment; you don't change your bets very often. In my 35 years in the business, there have been only a handful of tectonic shifts big enough and long-lasting enough to justify major asset allocation bets. One was the Carter period of rising inflation and increased tax rates—a good time to be out of stocks and bonds and into real estate. Falling inflation and lower tax rates during the Reagan years made domestic stocks and bonds the place to be. In the $1.3 trillion Resolution Trust Corporation (RTC) property deflation of 1990-93, it would have been smart to be out of real estate. The post-1990 collapse of the Japanese stock and real estate markets was a time to be out of Japanese investments. The dot-com boom, bubble and bust was another, as was the credit crunch that followed it. The 2003 dividend tax cut, the opening of China and the mortgage crisis can also join this list of tectonic shifts big enough—and long-lasting enough—to warrant major changes in asset mix.

Pretty simple. An investor who got all these right—about one decision every five years—would be reading this book on his own private beach.

But yesterday's trends are no help for today's investor. My asset allocation bet over the next few years would be to own large-cap U.S. stocks with plenty of exposure to Asia. I will talk about why in later chapters.

## Intrinsic Value

Investors own securities for one reason—they want to get paid. Stocks and bonds are simply claims on the future cash flow that the underlying assets on the company's balance sheet generate. The present value of those future free cash flow streams is the *Intrinsic Value* of the company and of its securities.

Over the past fifteen years, Deborah Allen and Paul Davis (my partners at Rutledge Research) and I have developed a set of forecasting models to estimate the intrinsic value of the U.S. stock market, its principal sectors, and individual stocks. We have used the model to identify situations in which stock prices were over- or undervalued.

Intrinsic value estimates are only as good as the estimates of the underlying business' value drivers—such as sales, price, cost, margins, tax rates, capital requirements and cost of capital—that are behind the calculations. These value drivers are strongly influenced by government policies.

From time to time, the interactions between buyers and sellers in the asset markets result in market prices that we find to be significantly above or below the intrinsic value of the securities. That's when stocks or bonds are overvalued or undervalued. Investors that consistently buy securities when they are undervalued and/or sell securities when they are overvalued will earn a higher after-tax return than other investors. It pays to do the work. I will discuss this—and other lessons I learned during my time in the private equity industry—in Chapter 5.

## Intrinsic Risk

Risk does not mean volatility; risk means losing your money. That happens when a business fails to deliver the operating performance that is embodied in the price an investor paid to acquire it. We call this *Intrinsic Risk*, and we measure it by explicitly estimating the probability that the value drivers that underlie a given market price will fail to deliver the expected free cash flow stream embodied in that price.

Wall Street is crazy for betas, which equate a stock's risk with its historical volatility relative to the market. I think betas are nonsense. No serious investor worries about volatility; they worry about losing their money.

There are two fundamentally different types of risk. *Market Risk* is the risk that you build a great business, but no buyer will pay you a fair price for it. Market risk is important for short periods but not meaningful for a patient investor who does his homework.

Intrinsic risk is when your initial judgment about a company's ability to generate sustainable free cash flow is wrong. You may have overestimated revenues or sales growth, underestimated costs, failed to anticipate capital needs, or had too high an opinion of the company's franchise or management. The bottom line is that it fails to deliver the sustainable growing cash flow you had anticipated in your intrinsic value estimate.

Intrinsic risk is much more important than market risk for investors. Patience won't make intrinsic risk go away. When investments die, it is almost always intrinsic risk that killed them.

## You Have to be Patient

The intrinsic value investor has two assistants to help him make money: Mr. Market and Mr. Momentum. Mr. Market is the wonderful fellow that Benjamin Graham and David Dodd wrote about over a half-century ago in their book *Security Analysis* (1934). He shows up at your door every day to give you a price at which he is happy to buy, and another price at which he would be happy to sell for every security in the market. He is quiet and sober. Most days his prices are fair—he will buy or sell a dollar of value for about one dollar. Most days the intrinsic value investor is not interested. Mr. Market is also polite; he will keep showing up every day even if you never do business with him. It's up to you.

Mr. Momentum is a different sort of guy. He tells you loudly what the smart investors are doing, and advises you to do the same while you still have time. When prices go up, he advises you to buy more. When they go down, he wants you to sell.

From time to time, Mr. Momentum pushes market prices far from their intrinsic values for long periods. This is when the intrinsic value investor makes his money.

Market prices exhibit a kind of tomcat stability. They wander away from home from time to time—sometimes a long ways away—and can be gone for months or even years at a time. But sooner or later, they always come home.

## Weather Map Investing

To me, a weather system is the best and simplest metaphor for economic change. We all know what happens when high and low pressure systems try to occupy the same space—thunder, lightning, tornadoes and hurricanes.

I think of global investing as an exercise in meteorology. My job is to identify the thermodynamic shifts—usually changes in tax rates, government spending, regulatory policies, or monetary policy—that lead to localized temperature or pressure differentials—price and return differentials—which, in turn, set up the arbitrage situations that we use to make money.

A change in zoning laws that alters cash flows, for example, creates a return differential that forces a change in the value of a piece of land. A tax law change that impacts after-tax returns leads to a return differential that forces a change in the value of a piece of capital equipment. A change in monetary policy that increases inflation increases the returns on tangible assets relative to securities, forcing a change in stock and bond prices. All can be viewed as weather systems moving across the weather map of the global economy.

I also like the weather map metaphor because it reminds me of two important facts. First, extraordinary investments, like weather systems, are all transitory phenomena. Even the best investments don't last forever.

Second, investing, like meteorology and thermodynamics, is not an exact science. It can help you to identify the storm systems that are going to make things happen. And it can tell you what things will look like when the storm has passed and thermal equilibrium has once again been restored. But it tells you nothing about what happens in between.

There is no exact science in either physics or economics that describes the disequilibrium states where change takes place. This is important for investing because all of the money is made and lost during the disequilibrium adjustment—nobody makes or loses money in equilibrium. That's why faith in the end result and the liquidity to withstand the turbulence and chaos along the way are so important.

The global weather map gives me a hat rack where I can hang the thousands of factoids that fill the news every day, so I can boil them all down to a manageable number of themes to watch closely.

The way to make money investing is to identify a storm system that is powerful enough, and likely to be long-lasting enough, to serve as an energy source for revaluing a portfolio. Then you move capital into position to take advantage of the implied prices changes. I will discuss this further later on in this chapter, and will discuss the link between recent work on information networks, recessions and credit crunches in Chapter 7.

## Storm Systems to Watch Today

These are some of the storm systems on my weather map today. I will discuss them briefly below.

### 2008 Elections

First the disclaimer. I am not a partisan; I am a principle-an. That means I will support any candidate, from any party, whose principles (if I am able to detect any) make sense to me. I decided long ago that I can't live with two masters—I can't always be loyal to my principles and to my tribe at the same time. I chose principles. Some people don't like that. They should learn to get used to disappointment.

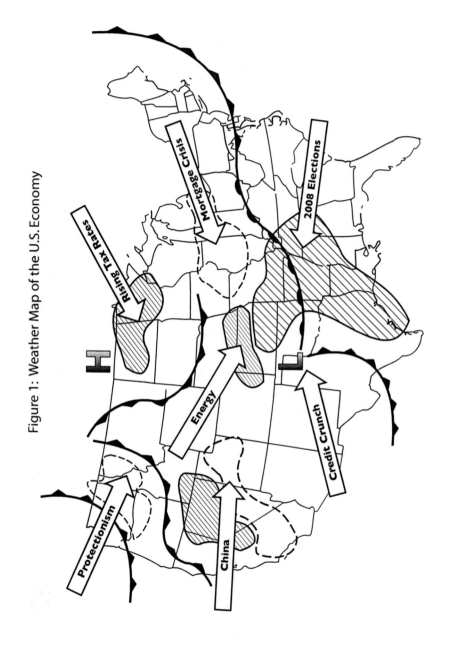

Figure 1: Weather Map of the U.S. Economy

I have often advised Republican administrations. I have also advised Democrats, the occasional monarchy and the People's Republic of China. Republican platforms often, but not always, support the ideas of personal liberty and limited government that I think are important; when they do I am on board. I do not like any government that exploits people's fears (about terrorism, about bird flu, about global warming) or anger (at the rich, at big oil companies, at immigrants, or at foreign workers) for political gain. This year's presidential election has plenty of both.

At the time of this writing, John McCain and Barack Obama are poised to take the stage in the November elections. This is an interesting time for the weather map investor, as the winner of the election will have a huge and immediate impact on the sorts of storm systems we can expect to see over the next four years.

### Rising Tax Rates

The most interesting difference between the two candidates for investors is tax policy. Senator McCain has indicated that he will support the extension of the 2003 reductions in the top marginal tax rates on ordinary income, dividends and capital gains. Senator Obama has indicated that he would support the expiration of the tax rates along with further increases, which would sharply increase tax rates on all three forms of income.

Tax rates are important for our weather map for a number of reasons. First, they impact incentives for work, saving and investment. Second, they're important for small businesses, which provide all new jobs; 80% of taxes collected at the top marginal tax rate are paid by small business owners. Third, changes in the tax rates on dividend income, capital gains and corporate profits drive wedges between the after-tax returns on some assets relative to others, setting up huge changes in asset prices.

### Protectionism

Protectionism is on the rise in America and has become an important topic in the 2008 presidential election. Protectionism is also growing in other countries. Ironically, as we will discuss in Chapter 6, rising protectionism may be a side effect of strong global growth.

Protectionist policies—tariffs, quotas, subsidies, currency bashing or restrictions on foreign investments—always lead to retaliation. The result is slower growth in both countries and declining stock prices. It will pay investors to keep an eye on trade policy during and after the election.

### Energy

Everyone agrees that high energy prices are bad for growth and increase the price level. Continued growth in China, India and other emerging economies will keep prices high for the foreseeable future. Not everyone agrees on what to do about it. Policies to increase supply (increased exploration and production, ethanol, alternative energy) or reduced demand (mileage standards, technology mandates) will have major implications for investors.

### Subprime Mortgage Crisis

Increased delinquencies on subprime mortgages, after years of rising home prices, caused a virtual blackout in the mortgage-backed securities market. As a result, prices have declined sharply in the last year, and the wipeout of construction spending has reduced 2008 GDP by one full percentage point. But blackouts always come to an end. And when they do, bond and stock prices will change in a hurry.

### Credit Crunch

Previous slowdowns have been triggered by sudden reductions in the availability of working capital for small, private companies. This time it's different. So far, lending problems have been concentrated in mortgages, asset-backed loans and large leveraged credits; business loans that provide working capital for the small companies that generate all new jobs have continued to grow. That's why GDP has continued to rise and employment has remained relatively stable. If the mortgage problem extends to business loans, the economy will be in trouble.

### United States–China Relations

The U.S. presidential elections and the Beijing Olympics ensure that U.S.-China relations will continue to be a front-page story all year. American voters are all aware of the issues, including product quality, trade, investment, Taiwan and Tibet—but few of them have enough first-hand experience to make reasoned judgments. This is ripe ground for political demagogues who prey on people's fears, and a great opportunity for those of us who have taken the time to get to know the people to help.

### Government Spending

The aging baby boomers and complete absence of political courage in Washington make today's Social Security and Medicare programs unsustainable. The prospect of universal health care legislation following this year's election would further worsen the problem.

*Climate Change and Green Power*

Projections of climate change have captured media attention as well as the political process. Congress will likely pass climate change legislation in the next year. The form of that legislation—whether taxes, subsidies, carbon trading schemes, regulations or unfunded mandates—will have major impacts on the profits and stock prices of different industries and sectors.

## There's No Room for Emotions in Investing

I know what you're thinking. "JR, if I follow your advice, on most days I'm not going to get to buy or sell *anything*! Shouldn't I be paying attention to the breaking news stories on TV all day?"

You should definitely pay attention to the news shows. After all, many of the producers and anchors are my friends and they need to make a living too. I watch the business news shows and read newspapers from all over the world every day so that I know everything that's happening. But you should never allow your emotions to influence your investment decisions. Every time I have done so, I have lost money.

Investing is not about emotion. It's about identifying situations where some assets will earn a higher return than others. Here are a few things to keep in mind when you watch the news.

Don't be distracted by the crisis *du jour*. The positive news on growth and profits always gets drowned out by a tsunami of breathless reports on oil prices, Iran, North Korea, trade, immigration, global warming, inflation and the Fed. That's why investors have been confused, frightened and sitting in cash. This is an emotional reaction, not a strategy. The world is not going to end, and we still need to educate our children and save enough so that we can eat when we are too old to work. This is when an investor needs the discipline to stay focused on long-term objectives, investment fundamentals, tax planning and a long-term strategy for building wealth.

Long-term investment fundamentals are actually strong. Productivity is rising and the U.S. economy is growing. Profits are growing and are at the highest percent of GDP ever recorded. Dividends are rising. The global economy is growing too, led by reforms in China and India. Capital owners have more choices of where to invest their money at attractive returns than ever before. The Fed and other central banks have shown that long-term inflation will be 1-2%. Bond yields are below 4% and likely to remain low. Stocks are cheap relative to projected earnings. These are great long-term fundamentals for equity markets.

Understand and manage risks, but don't let risk drive your investment strategy. China's growth has fundamentally changed world oil and commodity markets; high prices are here to stay. High oil prices have brought Iran, Russia, Venezuela and the Gulf Region back into the headlines. Home prices are falling. Protectionism is on the rise. Tax rates may go up.

Investment strategy should focus on long-term returns. Defensive strategies—extra cash, short bond maturities, defensive sectors—are okay in the short-term. But in the long-term, focus on high-quality U.S. companies with strong cash flows and rising dividends, and on countries, sectors and industries selling products and services to fast-growing Asia. I think U.S. stocks will produce upwards of 10% returns over the next five years, compared with 4% for bonds, 2% for cash and 0% for real estate. Asian equity markets will produce 10-15% returns—but don't chase hot commodity prices or Asian IPOs. And don't invest in places where you don't understand the law, the courts and the financial statements.

Diversification and tax planning still matter. I like to use ETFs to place small bets—less than 5% of the portfolio—on countries, regions, sectors, or industries where policy or technology change has raised after-tax returns on capital relative to the market. I reserve company bets for (rare) situations where I believe I have an information advantage over the market.

# 3

# Tangible Assets

W hen I arrived at Tulane University in 1973, I was a 23 year-old assistant professor with a new Ph.D. from the University of Virginia; I did not yet know most of the things I wrote about in the previous chapter. I knew that increasing the money supply causes inflation, and that inflation increases interest rates, but I didn't know why. I *thought* I knew that fiscal policy affected the economy through its impact on spending. I knew nothing about taxes, incentives and growth.

## Inflation Expectations

I had just finished writing my dissertation, which was soon to be published as *A Monetarist Model of Inflationary Expectations* (1973), about the impact of inflation on interest rates. When I dig for information, I

*Tulane University, 1973*

like to dig through the footnotes to get all the way down to the bottom.[1] So when I reviewed the economics literature on how inflation expectations are formed, I ended up studying John Locke's work on epistemology, or theory of learning, titled *An Essay Concerning Human Understanding* (1690). It was my first serious study of how the mind works, a field known today as cognitive science. As I will explore in Chapter 9, cognitive science is one of the most exciting areas of research going on today.

Although economists had written about inflation and interest rates, no one at the time had developed a model of how people form inflation expectations. So I built a model of the information market in order to analyze how investors decide what kinds of information to collect, how much of it to collect, and how to translate it into expecta-

---

[1] There is a modern term for this, of course: anal-retentive. My first attempt to understand interest rates was in 1969, when I wrote a senior thesis at Lake Forest College on money and interest rates. Since I knew nothing about interest rates, I thought the most obvious approach was to find the relevant section in the library, begin with the book on the top left shelf, and read until I reached the lower right-hand corner of the section. I decided that I needed to have a regression in my thesis measuring the impact of changes in money supply on interest rates. The problem was, I had never studied econometrics, there was no regression program, and we didn't have a computer. So I did the obvious thing. I found an abandoned IBM 360 that the college had once used to print payroll, found the user manuals in a desk drawer and the on/off switch on the back of the machine, read about source code, object code and punch cards, and turned it on. There was no regression software, so I learned how to program in Fortran and figured out how to do the regression from a statistics book. Then I gathered the data, wrote the regression program, punched the cards, compiled the program, ran the program and printed the results. Altogether, it took a year of work to estimate one regression equation. Today, I can do it in between sips of coffee. Now that's progress!

tions. I used the model to test the then-controversial theory of rational expectations, which essentially says that there is no reason to presume that investors are dumber than academic economists. (Now, there's an understatement.)

## 1970s Inflation

In 1975, I met a wonderful mon-etary economist named James Meigs who was about to join the economics faculty of Claremont Men's College (CMC)—now Claremont McKenna College—to start an economic fore-casting institute. I moved to CMC too, and we got to work. Jim was a former student of Milton Friedman and a vet-eran of Citibank's economics opera-tion; he taught me a lot about the fi-nancial markets. Together, we advised dozens of financial institutions in the 1970s.

*Claremont Men's College, 1984*

In the late 1970s, Jimmy Carter was president. Inflation, tax rates, government spending and interest rates were all rising, and growth was stagnant. Real estate and commodity prices were soaring. The stock and bond markets were a mess, and the dollar was dropping like a brick.

Accepted wisdom at the time was that inflation was not a prob-lem for the real economy. After all, labor and product contracts could be indexed; interest rates would rise by just enough to compensate sav-ers for their expected loss of purchasing power—a view mistakenly at-tributed to the great economist Irving Fisher—leaving real interest rates unchanged.[2] In fact, most economists accepted the now discredited Phillips Curve notion that rising inflation actually *increases* growth. Accepted wisdom was not doing a very good job of explaining the 1970s.

## Tangible Assets

In 1978, I found an extraordinary set of data on the public's asset holdings. Actually, it found me. Jim Meigs, Jerry St. Dennis and I were doing a project called *Study of World Economic Change* with William Simon and Booz Allen Hamilton. My part was to build an interlinked econometric model of the 10 major economies—we called it GlobeSim—so that we could explain to the heads of 50 multinational corporations (who knew way more about it than I did) how the new world of flexible exchange rates worked.

One of our clients was the Northwestern Mutual Life Insurance Company (NML) in Milwaukee, Wisconsin. One day while I was explaining how the world worked, Harvey Wilmeth, a very smart man—one of the NML executives and a chemical engineer by training—kept (politely) asking me questions I didn't know how to answer. He had made a detailed study of U.S. tangible wealth, and concluded it was very important.

Later, at lunch, Harvey showed me the Federal Reserve Board's *Balance Sheet of the United States*, which reported the market value of people's holdings of tangible assets—land, houses, capital goods, consumer durables and commodities—in addition to the figures for financial assets—deposits, stocks and bonds—that I already knew about. Tangible assets—all of the stuff you see when you look out of an airplane window—were *huge*, bigger than anything macroeconomists were writing about at the time. But I had no idea why they mattered.

---

[2] Fisher—like Knut Wicksell, John Maynard Keynes, Joseph Schumpeter, Ludwig von Mises and Eugen von Böhm-Bawerk—understood the lessons of the periodic deflations and financial panics that had plagued Western countries through the 1930s. Monetary, credit and tax disturbances have major effects on both real interest rates and on real economic activity.

What intrigued me most was that macroeconomics had no analytical pigeonhole for this data. In a flow chart contained in his 1971 presidential address to the American Economic Association, James Tobin identified "the interest rate" simply as a parameter set by the central bank. Asset arbitrage—which Tobin's followers later had the hubris to call "Modern Portfolio Theory"—was confined to financial markets. Interest rates influenced the production economy through their effects on investment decisions, but the real economy did not influence interest rates. Real assets, at least as far as the model was concerned, did not exist.

How could that be, I wondered? Interest rates were simply prices of a particular subset of people's assets. The largest asset class was actually real estate, not securities. It sounded like the joke going around about the U.S. government's refusal to recognize the one billion people in China: How could we ignore our biggest asset?

My colleagues and I at the Claremont Economics Institute (CEI) used this data to build a new model of the economy based on the idea that people change their holdings of tangible and financial assets when they have incentives to do so. Inflation increased the return on tangible assets, but not on financial assets. Increased tax rates reduced the after-tax return on financial assets, but not on tangible assets. Both gave people incentives to shift wealth from financial assets to hard assets.

This framework unified the behavior of the hard asset markets with the security markets, and explained why variations in inflation and tax rates exert powerful real effects on interest rates, asset values and real wealth accumulation.

We used this model to great profit during the later stages of the Carter inflation to predict the effects of rising inflation and tax rates on interest rates and commodity prices.

In 1980, we used the framework to develop scenarios to illustrate what would happen to the economy if different candidates won the 1980 election. We initially wrote a report detailing Reagan and Kennedy scenarios. Later, of course, it became the Reagan-Carter scenario. Each scenario was based on an economic plan constructed to fit the candidate. The Reagan scenario was based on economic policies of reduced government spending, reduced tax rates, deregulation and support for the Fed's lower inflation policy. These policies, we reasoned, would initially lead to a sharp slowdown of the economy but, over time, would push inflation and interest rates much lower. We used it to develop business and investment strategies for our clients.

We didn't know it at the time, but several of our clients were also friends and advisors of Ronald Reagan. They were sending our material to him during the campaign. We did know, however, that Reagan had seen our work personally. Once, when candidate Reagan made a stump speech in the Claremont city park, my trusted partner Deborah Allen broke through the line of Secret Service agents and placed a copy of our plan in Reagan's hands.

The week after the election, I received a call from President Reagan's transition team asking if I would like to come to Washington and help draft the Reagan economic plan. My friend Larry Kudlow, then at Paine-Webber, had given us a big push when he got a visit from David Stockman, whom Reagan had put in charge of writing his new economic plan. Together we invaded Washington to help write the plan that critics dubbed "Rosy Scenario."

Twenty-eight years later, Rosy still looks beautiful to me. In 1981, when President Reagan announced his economic plan, inflation was 15% and the (federal) top marginal tax rate was 70%, which had turned Americans into a nation of tax shelter and inflation hedge experts rather than investors, entrepreneurs and workers. Instead of buying financial assets like stocks, bonds and mutual funds, they bought tangible assets like commodities, farmland and gold coins. Instead of starting businesses, they developed shopping centers. Instead of working, they borrowed to buy real estate they did not need.

By 1981, tangible assets like these exceeded 43% of people's total assets, up from less than 30% through most of history. To accomplish this, they dumped financial assets—which pushed short-term interest rates above 20%, long-term Treasury yields over 15%, and reduced stock market multiples to single digits.

Now, almost thirty years later, all this has been turned on its head. Reagan's low inflation and low marginal tax rates undercut the return on tax and inflation shelters and enhanced the after-tax return on securities. In response, Americans shifted 11% of total assets, roughly $11 trillion, out of tangible assets and into securities. This $11 trillion arbitrage event has profoundly affected every one of our economic lives. In the face of such powerful forces of change, ordinary macroeconomic issues concerning budget and trade deficits were simply brushed aside.

Hard asset prices collapsed and financial asset prices soared. This dramatic increase in the value of a dollar of future income manifested itself in lower interest rates and higher valuation multiples. A $100,000 investment in the synthetic equivalent of 30-year zero-coupon treasury bonds in August 1981 would be worth over $2,000,000 today—more than 20 times your initial investment.

These asset market events had important effects on the production economy as well. Hard asset deflation made the carrying cost of low-return assets too heavy for U.S. companies to bear. American industry embarked on a ruthless decade-long restructuring wave that left U.S. companies lean and mean. Falling interest rates and rising stock multiples reduced the after-tax cost of capital for American companies investing in new, high-return assets. The end result was a tidal wave of investment and innovation that improved efficiency and lowered costs for American companies. Low tax rates created powerful work incentives. Together, these factors returned the U.S. to its former position as the preeminent economic power in the world.

## Why Interest Rates Will Fall in 1982

Our tangible asset framework had its public debut in November 1981, when I wrote an Op-Ed for the *Wall Street Journal* called "Why Interest Rates Will Fall in 1982." At that time, Wall Street was divided between people like Dr. Doom and Mr. Gloom: those who believed Reagan's tax cuts would lead to big budget deficits, and therefore rising interest rates; and those who argued that Reagan's tax cuts would stimulate more savings and therefore drive interest rates down.

I had described the tangible asset analysis to Irving Kristol, political scientist at the American Enterprise Institute, on a cocktail napkin in the bar of the New York Athletic Club a few weeks earlier. Irving said he thought it was an important idea that should be published in the *Wall Street Journal.* He called Bob Bartley, editor of the *Journal,* the same day. I owe both of them a large thank you. Years later, Bob Bartley wrote a wonderful book called *The Seven Fat Years* which reviewed the events surrounding the major policy decisions of the 1980s. In the book, Bob referred to this analysis with very kind words. Irving Kristol and Bob Bartley, along with Charlie Parker, the man who introduced me to Irving and has been my best friend ever since, are the most curious and intellectually honest men I have ever known.

I argued in the article that the course of interest rates would not depend on savings or deficits. Instead, the Reagan Administration's economic plan contained inflation and tax rate reductions that were going to turn the asset markets on their head by forcing massive private sector asset arbitrage. These arbitrage activities would lead to a reversal of all the major trends of the 1970s. Interest rates had to fall, regardless of the budget deficit or the savings rate. Deficits and savings rates would be rounding errors in the biggest portfolio event of the century.

I didn't get many dinner invitations from fellow economists after that. But the investors I advised did make a lot of money. Here are a few of the arguments from that article.

—

It is now said that the federal deficit for fiscal 1982 will be roughly $100 billion. This has sparked a furious debate on Wall Street between analysts who say that such large government borrowing must push interest rates higher; and supply-siders, who believe tax cut-induced increases in household savings will more than offset rising government borrowing needs, and hence must push interest rates lower.

Both sides of the debate use a flow-of-funds framework to forecast interest rates. This framework views a financial market as a kind of farmers' market, where households bring their savings (credit supplies) and governments and corporations bring their borrowing needs (credit demands). Interest rates are the price that equates credit demands and credit supplies. This is the source of the current fixation on deficits and savings.

Wall Streeters fear that mega-deficits will piggyback the growing calendar of corporate debt issues to explode credit demands. Savings won't be able to increase fast enough to meet these needs. After a brief dip, due to the recession, short-term interest rates will climb to new highs by late 1982.

Supply-siders believe the tax cut will increase the after-tax real rate of return on investment income, inducing households to increase savings. These increased savings, they argue, will provide more than enough credit to satisfy government and corporate appetites for funds, letting interest rates fall during 1982.

In my view, […] major changes in U.S. interest rates are usually caused by changes in the way the public wants to hold its net worth.

The drop in inflation in the last 18 months is forcing households to restructure their wealth in a way that will force reductions in interest rates in 1982, no matter what the level of savings or budget deficits in the next year.

In adopting the flow-of-funds framework of interest rate forecasting, both sides neglect the fact that, in addition to owning stocks, bonds, bank accounts, money market certificates and other financial assets, households also own condominiums, land, used cars, gold and countless other tangible assets. This stock of existing goods or tangible assets has been produced and stockpiled over many years, and in a real sense represents the nation's collected real wealth.

The stock of tangible assets in the U.S. is enormous. At today's prices, the total stock of houses, cars, collectibles and other tangibles is worth about $7 trillion. That's more than twice the total value of the goods and services the U.S. economy will produce this year.

Failing to recognize the existence of the stocks of tangible assets renders flow-of-funds analysis almost worthless for forecasting interest rates.

To private investors, tangible assets are substitutes, or alternatives, to financial assets […]. To consumers, tangible assets are substitutes for buying currently produced goods and services. Since the amounts in question are so huge—$7 trillion—even a moderate shift in the way households want to hold assets can have a huge effect on both credit markets and durable goods sales.

The key to understanding the influence of tangible assets on interest rates is the concept of "asset market equilibrium." An individual is free to hold his wealth in any combination of assets he chooses. [...] Asset market equilibrium describes the state in which each asset holder is holding the combination of assets which, at current market prices, he finds most desirable.

What happens if people desire more condominiums than exist? Individuals bidding for that scarce supply would drive the price higher, and the attempted sale of bonds or other securities to fund the condo purchases would tend to force securities prices down. These price changes tend to lower the yield on condos as an investment and raise the yield on bonds, causing people to reconsider their initial choices. Ultimately, both condo and security prices settle at levels which, again, make people content to hold the existing stock of assets.

This is not a new idea. James Tobin just received the Nobel Prize in economics for developing the notion of portfolio balance. Mr. Tobin's idea was that the prices (interest rates) of financial assets will go to whatever level will make investors just content to hold the available stock of those assets. All we have done is to add tangible assets—land and so forth—to the portfolio management problem faced by every household.

This addition radically changes the nature of financial analysis and interest rate forecasting. It breaks the link between savings and credit supplies that plays such an important role in the flow-of-funds framework.

A household that owns tangible assets can supply credit in two distinct ways: 1) by increasing savings, i.e., buying securities, out of its current income, or 2) selling [...] tangible assets to buy [securities]. The results are the same: increased credit supplies and lower interest rates.

A general increase in the public's desire to hold financial assets—a desire to exchange tangible assets for financial assets—plays the role of an increase in credit supplies. Since the public's holdings of both tangible assets and financial assets are extremely large, a relatively minor change in their desired asset mix can overwhelm the effect of savings and budget deficits on interest rates.

The following graph shows how people changed their holdings of tangible assets as the inflation rate varied during the 1970s.

## Figure 2: Private Tangible Assets and Inflation

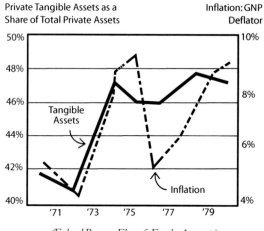

*(Federal Reserve Flow of Funds Accounts)*

This evidence suggests that each percentage point drop in the inflation rate should send about one percent of people's tangible assets back into the financial markets as increased credit supplies. Inflation in 1982 (6%) should be about four percentage points lower than 1981; this suggests we'll see an increase in credit supplies of

$400–$500 billion. No one has yet predicted that the deficit will hit one-half trillion dollars for 1982. If it does not, interest rates must fall.

—

To my delight, this article stimulated a spirited debate in the pages of the *Wall Street Journal*. The debate continued in the *Wall Street Journal*, *Barron's*, *Forbes*, *Fortune*, the *New York Times* and the *Financial Times* during the first half of the 1980s. It was a career-building event for me.

Does the idea still work? The Reagan story played out some time ago but the same logic can be applied to any other situation where a policy or technology change drives a wedge between the after-tax return on one large category of assets relative to returns on other assets. Examples include Japan's lost decade of the 1990s when deflation imploded its economy, the technology surge of the late 1990s, and the entry of China into the global capital market.

## Supply-Side Balance Sheet Economics

My friend Arthur Laffer— referred to as one of the founding fathers of supply-side economics alongside my friend Bob Mundell—asked me to write an article outlining the links between the U.S. balance sheet and supply-side economics. It was a great chance to work with an old friend

*Art Laffer, Inventor of the Laffer Curve*

that I respect tremendously, both personally and professionally, and to think more deeply about the links between the economy's income statement, which measures GDP, and its balance sheet, or wealth.

That got me thinking about the parallels between arbitrage— whether between products or assets—and thermodynamics. This put us in good company; both Albert Einstein and Richard Feynman described thermodynamics as the only laws they believed would hold for all time. Together, the concepts of arbitrage and thermodynamics provide us with an alternative to traditional macroeconomics. You will learn more about this in Chapter 6.

## What's Wrong With Macroeconomics

In macroeconomics classes all across America, students learn that governments can control the economy by manipulating spending and tax rates. They learn about the Phillips Curve, which claims that more growth leads to inflation, which then leads to the nonsensical conclusion that the act of working creates inflation. They learn that interest rates are determined by the Federal Reserve, by budget deficits and by flows of funds between savers and investors, rather than the portfolio decisions of wealth holders. Worst of all, they learn that our collective wealth and standard of living are determined by how much money we spend, not by how hard we work, what we create, or how much we save and invest. Students should really be learning about arbitrage and thermodynamics.

Macroeconomics textbooks begin with a hypothetical island economy. Some people on the island catch fish, the story goes, and others pick coconuts. They exchange fish and coconuts with each other (so they get all two major food groups) using a barter system. The island's GDP is the sum of the fish and coconuts produced in a year. Since both fish and coconuts are perishable—you catch it, you eat it—GDP also equals total consumption for the year. Savings and investment both equal zero. There are no capital markets—no assets—in the island economy; therefore, no interest rates. It is not possible to produce in one period and consume in the next.

The great French economist Maurice Allais (1947) introduced the idea of assets to the island economy by allowing its inhabitants to make handshake IOUs, effectively saying, "If you allow me to eat some of the fish and coconuts that you produce this year, I will promise to al-

## Figure 3: The Island Economy

low you to eat some of the fish and coconuts I produce next year." In doing so, Allais showed that certain demographic patterns could result in a negative real interest rate. People near retirement age, for example, have incentives to "save" by feeding young people today who will, in turn, feed them when they are too old to work. If there are many people near retirement-age relative to young workers, an old worker may have to pay a young worker two coconuts today to get one coconut back in the future—a real (coconut) interest rate of negative 50%.

The interesting questions of capital markets only arise, however, when there are many assets, when real goods are storable, and when people are able to make choices among alternative ways to store wealth. I actually live part of the time on an island—Maui—so I know something about island economies. There are fish in the ocean in front of my house and coconuts in the back yard, just like in the textbooks. When I go to sleep every night, however, I don't worry about the fish or the coconuts. I worry about the volcano the island is sitting on. If it erupts during the night, tomorrow is going to be a very bad day.

Our $14 trillion U.S. economy sits on top of a volcano too—its $200 trillion balance sheet. Even small disturbances in such a huge base of assets can set up forces—thermal disequilibria, in physics terms—so large that they swamp the effects of the changes in spending, savings, budget deficits and other "flow" measures from macroeconomics. These tidal waves of change are transmitted to people's lives through changes in asset prices.

## Two Price Theories

As economists, we have two theories about prices. The first— supply and demand—is the price theory of Alfred Marshall (1890) and George Stigler (1946). It works well for haircuts, guitar lessons and other perishable goods and services, which are all things with big current production and small stockpiles. The second price theory—portfolio theory—is associated with Irving Fisher (1896) and James Tobin (1958). It works for long-lasting goods like Rembrandts, '57 Chevys and beachfront property.

Most products are *somewhat* storable but wear out over time. We should analyze the prices of medical services, food and apparel, for example, using supply and demand. We should analyze the prices of land, homes, copper, gold and even automobiles (there were 191 million used vehicles in the U.S. in 2001) as assets. Bond prices behave like Maui beachfront. For example, at the end of 2007 there were $9.4 trillion in outstanding debt obligations of the federal government, $5.4 trillion of which was held by the public. By comparison, the total federal budget deficit for 2007 was just over $350 billion. Investors already held $15.40 of government bonds in their portfolios for each $1.00 of new debt sold during the year. A bond is an asset, not a good or a service; it should be analyzed that way.

This means that the supply of bonds is, for all practical purposes, invariant to price—the supply curve is vertical. Put another way, bond prices—and therefore interest rates—will be insensitive to government financing activities. Interest rates are determined by the structure of asset demand; they will be whatever they need to be to make people hold the existing stock of bonds.

## U.S. Balance Sheets are Huge

The U.S. asset markets are huge. At the end of 2007, the Federal Reserve Board reported total U.S. *financial* assets of $141.9 trillion,[3] equal to 10.3 times 2007 GDP of $13.8 trillion. In addition, the Fed reported $50.0 trillion in tangible asset holdings by households, nonprofits, corporations and private companies (not counting farms or any level of government).[4]

The household sector alone owned $26.8 trillion worth of tangible assets, including $22.5 trillion in real estate and $4.0 trillion in durable goods—used cars, boats, furniture, clothes and iPods. Businesses owned another $22.5 trillion in tangible assets, including $4.6 trillion in equip-

---

[3]   *Flow of Funds Statement*, Fourth Quarter, 2007.
[4]   The GAO reports that the federal government alone owns more than 700 million acres of land. They are not reported at all on the federal government balance sheet on the theory that the government is merely holding them in trust for future generations. I am going to try that trick next year when the IRS asks me to report the gains on my assets as income. "What assets? I am merely holding these stocks in trust for my children."

ment and software and $1.9 trillion of inventories. Household net worth was a whopping $55.7 trillion.

## Asset Market Equilibrium

Asset market equilibrium takes place when prices are at levels such that there are no arbitrage opportunities—no return differentials—for investors to exploit. Anything that materially alters the relative risks or returns will tilt the scale, leading investors to adjust portfolios toward the relatively high return assets. This shift forces asset prices, and therefore returns, to change until investors are once again content to own the existing assets and equilibrium has been restored.

The reason it is a good idea to split the national balance sheet into tangible versus financial assets is that the two major policy instruments—inflation and tax rates—affect their returns so differently. Inflation adds capital gains to the return on tangible assets, which is why inflation causes investors to sell securities and shift their portfolios toward tangible assets. Doing so drives tangible asset prices up and financial asset prices down, i.e., interest rates up, until equilibrium is restored.

Similarly, an increase in tax rates reduces the relative after-tax return of financial assets because the yield on tangible assets—the value of living in your house—is not taxed. So, an increase in tax rates shifts asset demand toward tangible assets, drives their prices up and drives financial asset prices down, until balance is once again restored.

Figure 4 offers a real-world example. The figure shows the relative price of stocks in terms of homes, which is calculated by dividing the market value of a portfolio of stocks (1,000 shares of the S&P 500 index) by the median price of an existing home. This ratio serves as a measure of household decisions concerning the composition of their portfolio between financial assets, in the form of shares of stock, and tangible assets, in the form of existing homes.

## Figure 4: Relative Price of Financial Assets to Tangible Assets

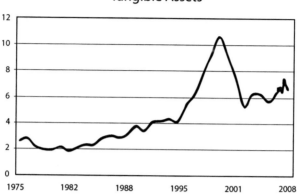

Stocks were valued at roughly two median homes in 1981, but increased to four homes by 1996. They peaked at more than eight homes during the dot-com boom in late 1999, later falling to less than six homes in early 2003 before the dividend and capital gains tax cuts. Stocks stand at about seven homes in mid-2008. With the exception of the dot-com period, the rising value of stocks in relation to real estate in the last 25 years made stocks a much better investment over this period. With falling housing prices due to the subprime mortgage crisis, stocks will continue to be the better choice in the next few years.

## Tangible Real Rate

Irving Fisher wrote about these concepts more than a century ago, when he examined the link between inflation and interest rates. John Maynard Keynes understood it as well; Chapter 17 of his *General Theory* is the most elegant description of asset arbitrage ever written. Asset arbitrage explains why real asset prices should be used to benchmark inflation, not consumer prices or GDP deflators, because the spread between tangible and financial asset yields is the key driver of investor behavior. Measured properly, this tangible real rate is the economic analog to the temperature differential that serves as the fundamental driver of change in thermodynamics.

Asset market disturbances are one-trick ponies, even big ones like the ones I have been describing. Much like hurricanes, when they are over, they are over. That leaves investors with two things to do: clean up the mess left by the storm—today it is the subprime mortgage mess—and start watching out for the next one.

# 4

## Budget Deficits

*A simple guide to understanding how budget deficits impact interest rates*

### Budget Deficits Do Not Determine Interest Rates

In spite of what the textbooks tell you, throughout history, the correlation between interest rates and deficits is actually negative; i.e., higher deficits are associated with lower interest rates. The drawings in this chapter explain why.

Interest rates are not determined by savings rates and are not determined by the demand for credit. As a logical matter, it is *debt*, not deficits, along with people's relative demand for assets, that determines interest rates.

Budget deficits in the ranges we usually see them don't matter much for the economy. Not for interest rates. Not for growth. The multitrillion dollar bond markets don't care at all whether the government is a net seller or a net buyer of $100 billion in new Treasury securities in a given year. They care whether the people who own the old paper today are still going to want to own it tomorrow. And that will depend on whether something happens to change their minds about future after-tax returns on bonds relative to other assets. The rest is all rounding errors. Nothing else matters.

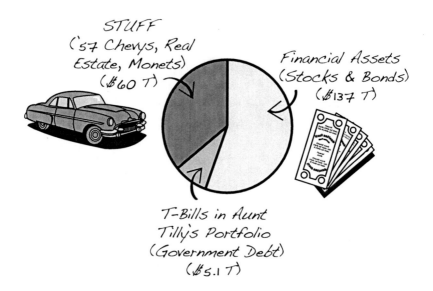

People's Total Assets

STUFF
('57 Chevys, Real Estate, Monets)
($60 T)

Financial Assets
(Stocks & Bonds)
($137 T)

T-Bills in Aunt Tilly's Portfolio
(Government Debt)
($5.1 T)

When the Treasury holds an auction to finance a deficit, they print and sell new T-bills or other Treasury IOUs to investors like Aunt Tilly. This isn't the first time the government has borrowed money from private citizens. Aunt Tilly and other investors already own a huge stock of similar old T-bills—$5.1 trillion worth at the end of 2007—that we call the national debt. At the end of last year, there were $9.2 trillion of old T-bills outstanding—the government's accumulated borrowing since the time of George Washington. Of those, $5.1 trillion, or 55%, was held by private investors like you, Aunt Tilly and me.

New treasury paper and old treasury paper are perfect substitutes to investors. Not *almost* perfect substitutes—*perfect* substitutes. In practice, they are indistinguishable in the market.[1] When you buy a bond, you shop for its issuer, its maturity date, its call provisions, its tax features, and its yield—not its model year. This means that new bonds and old bonds that are the same in every other way *must* sell at the same price. Arbitrageurs make sure they do.

It's like the commercial where the dad asks his teenage son to drive to the local gas station to put gas in the family car. Hours later, the dad is still standing in the driveway when his son returns with the explanation, "But Dad, you didn't want me to mix the new gas with the old gas, did you?"

Bond investors mix the new bonds with the old bonds all the time.

Flow-of-funds is a theory to explain the price of *new* bonds. Portfolio balance is a theory to explain the price of *old* bonds. But in the real world, there can only be *one* price for *all* bonds. Which theory wins? Portfolio balance, because almost all bonds are old bonds. The important question is not whether the government will borrow money this year. It is what price it will take to make Aunt Tilly—and all the other investors who owned T-bills yesterday—still want to own the stock of T-bills tomorrow.

But balance sheets do not sit still; they grow over time. The stock of tangible assets grows as a result of building houses, factories, shopping centers and new cars faster than they wear out. The stock of private financial assets grows as people issue mortgages to finance home purchases, and companies issue new stocks and bonds to finance capital spending, home construction and durable goods production—at a faster rate than the old ones mature. We create new government securities to

---

[1]  T-bills, notes and bonds are also very good substitutes for many other securities owned by investors, including agency securities, corporate securities, municipal securities and securities issued by financial institutions. These, in turn, are substitutes to some degree for equities, foreign securities and tangible assets in the minds of investors.

finance the budget deficit, or we destroy them by using a budget surplus to buy back debt.

As our net worth grows, so does our appetite to hold *all* assets. This growth is represented by drawing a second pie chart showing the larger stock of stuff (tangible assets) and financial assets. Historically, U.S. balance sheets have grown at about 7% per year.

## Next Year's Total Asset Growth

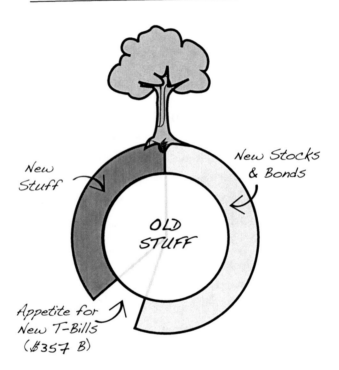

New Stuff

New Stocks & Bonds

OLD STUFF

Appetite for New T-Bills ($357 B)

Higher net worth gives investors like Aunt Tilly an appetite to own more T-Bills too, as illustrated in the drawing. You can think of this appetite as thousands of Aunt Tillys standing in line in front of the Treasury building, waiting to place orders for the new T-bills that the government will sell next year (to add to the ones they already own).

That appetite is larger than most people think. If net worth grows 7% next year, as it has done historically, investors will want to increase their holdings of T-bills by $357 billion, from $5.1 trillion to just under $5.5 trillion.

If the Treasury issues just enough new T-bills to satisfy Aunt Tilly's appetite, then everyone will go away happy. There will be just enough T-bills to go around. Prices will remain the same as they were last year. Interest rates will remain unchanged.

But what would happen if the treasury issued too few or too many T-bills to satisfy investors' appetites? That's easy. There would be a scuffle.

If they were too few T-Bills for sale due to a smaller government deficit, then Aunt Tilly would wrestle with the other investors for the limited supply. This would drive T-Bill prices up and interest rates down.

## Too Few New T-Bills

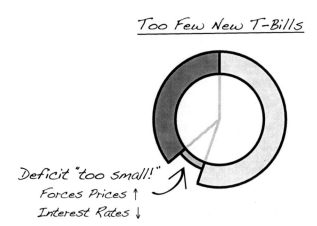

Deficit "too small!"
Forces Prices ↑
Interest Rates ↓

If the government ran up the deficit and there were too many T-Bills for sale, then the Treasury would be forced to lower their asking price to sell their inventory. T-Bill prices would fall and interest rates would rise.

*Too Many New T-Bills*

*Deficit "too BIG!"*
*Forces Prices ↓*
*Interest Rates ↑*

It is only to the extent that budget deficits exceed Aunt Tilly's appetite for new securities that they can be said to push interest rates up at all. In our example, we can think of the $357 billion from the previous example as the *interest rate neutral budget deficit*—one that will put no pressure on interest rates. The balanced budget that we all wish for would actually exert downward pressure on interest rates every year. Over time, government debt would gradually become extinct like the dodo bird; it would be irrelevant for investors.

This does not mean that I love budget deficits. It does not mean that deficits are good or bad. And it does not blunt the fact that higher government spending uses tons of resources and creates all sorts of incentive and resource allocation problems. It just means that budget deficits are unlikely to be a factor in determining interest rates in the range in which we are likely to see them.

If deficits don't determine interest rates, then what does? The answer is any factor that could drive a wedge between the relative returns on different assets. Higher inflation does that by increasing the return on tangible assets relative to securities. That makes people sell securities to increase their holdings of real assets, like we saw during the 1970s, which drives interest rates higher. Lower income tax rates increase the after-tax returns on taxable securities relative to real assets, for which income is generally not reported or taxed. This will drive interest rates lower. Rising productivity growth can quicken net worth growth, which will increase Aunt Tilly's appetite for all assets and drive interest rates lower. And the Fed can influence the rate of net worth growth by making it easier or more difficult to finance investments.

## Budget Bucks

These days everyone seems to have his own remedy for the ballooning federal budget deficit. The cures range from Balanced Budget Amendments, spending freezes, and program cuts to 50 ways to raise your taxes. All are attempts to impose some sort of discipline on the actions of a group of entirely undisciplined hooligans (a.k.a. members of Congress).

Since Congress has not managed to come up with a way to provide internal discipline—roughly equivalent to slipping into your own straitjacket—the capital markets have responded with external discipline. The usual positive spread between the yields on bonds and Treasury bills can be interpreted, at least in part, as the country's investment managers giving the government failing marks in fiscal discipline.

The trouble with most existing proposals for fiscal discipline is that they are either directed at the budget process, like the Balanced Budget Amendment, and imply all sorts of administrative problems, or they are directed at shrinking existing programs, which gets into all sorts of political problems. Nobody has yet come up with an easy-to-use procedure that is only concerned with the budget totals, not with specific programs. What we need is a proposal that operates in an even way on the outlay side of the budget, while not goring anyone's particular ox and not creating 19 new committees and two tons of new red tape a week.

I have one such modest proposal. My proposal is stolen from the ultimate practitioners of fiscal discipline, the international currency markets. In the currency markets, when one country does a particularly bad job of handling its internal finances, the currency traders turn on the country in question like piranha and savage its money. This is a way of containing the disease before it can spread to other countries and their monies.

This system also has the Calvinistic advantage of making those who were responsible for the problem pay for it by seeing their money shrink in buying power while still in their pockets. Eventually, this—like the two-by-four and the mule—gets their attention and encourages them to behave in a more responsible manner. In fact, it was just such a humiliating shellacking of the dollar in the fall of 1979 that allowed Paul Volcker to bring our inflation rate down to today's level.

I think we should apply the same logic to federal spending. We need a simple way to devalue the government's budget whenever Congress' appetite for programs extends beyond its ability to pay for them. For guidelines, it should be simple and quick, and it should make those who are responsible for excessive government spending, i.e. the special interest lobby groups, bear the brunt of any costs.

The answer is Budget Bucks (BBs). I propose that we leave the tax side of the budget alone and continue collecting taxes more or less as we do now—with taxpayers sending real money to the Treasury Department, which holds the money to pay its bills.

The difference is on the outlay side of the budget. I propose that anyone who gets paid by the government, whether for wages, for making tanks, or for doing nothing (welfare), should receive budget bucks instead of real money. Budget bucks would be a special new kind of money used by the government to pay its bills, but which are not—repeat, *not*—legal tender in grocery stores, lumberyards and liquor stores across the land. My design for budget bucks is shown in the accompanying illustration. They should be small. They should be red in color. And they should be engraved with the ever-imposing image of Uncle Sam. (We want YOU to be fiscally responsible!)

If BBs are not legal tender, then how can anyone use them to pay their bills? Simple. Make the budget bucks convertible into real money at the local post office. By now, of course, you are saying to yourself, "Of course, the budget savings are obvious. Simply distribute all government outlays through the post office in the form of BBs. That way, the post office will surely lose at least 20% of the checks, and at least another 20% will be seriously delayed, resulting in a minimum savings of 40% in the first year." That is not, however, the savings I am writing about.

Then how does it help the budget deficit? Simply set the rate of exchange of BBs and real money at a level that varies day-to-day to accomplish the level of spending, when measured in real money, which exactly equals government revenues. That way, regardless of the number of grand government programs that are invented and installed by Congress, the budget, in real American dollars, will always be in balance.

For example, if the government overpromises—known as over-booking in the airline industry—and spends two dollars for each one dollars it takes in as taxes (a situation which, in light of recent history, is not too farfetched), then each BB brought to the post office will be worth only 50 cents. The Treasury buys back the BBs from the post office at the discount price and presto, the budget, in real money, is balanced. No balancing problems, no constitutional conventions, no political maneuvering—just smaller budget bucks.

The flexi-budget idea simply works like a reducing Xerox machine to deflate the outlay sides of the budget by just enough to fit inside the available revenues of the government. This is nothing more than a way to make operative the "cut the coat to fit the cloth" rhetoric that we heard so much about from President Reagan in 1981.

The budgeting benefits of the plan are apparent—the government would never borrow money again. In fact, by setting the balanced budget value of BBs at a slight discount, the Treasury could use the BB scheme to generate enough revenues to pay off or amortize the current amount of the national debt over whatever future period they wished. I know that paying off the national debt is a radical idea, last practiced by Treasury secretary Andrew Mellon in the 1920s and briefly by President Clinton in the late 1990s, but what the heck—as long as we're proposing solutions, let's not be timid.

The real payoff to my proposal is what it would do to political incentives. It would turn everyone living at the public trough into a fiscal conservative. In the current system, all a special interest lobby cares about is whether they get the money they're after—they couldn't care less about the size and number of other government programs. After all, there is plenty of room for all at the public trough.

Under my proposal, every time a new program is laid on, the trough gets a little smaller for all those currently living on the dole. People receiving money from the government would have an active interest in using their influence to get Congress to spend less money on all programs other than their own. That's the only way they can be sure that the BBs they have lobbied so long and hard for will have any real money value when they cash them in.

For example, Social Security recipients will begin leaning on their congressmen to spend less on defense, defense contractors will begin leaning on their congressmen to spend less on welfare, and both will lean on their congressmen to reduce congressional pension payments. This turn in the political tables can only make the budget smaller—even when measured in BBs. Who knows, maybe the born-again anti-spending lobbies would be so effective that there would be a surplus in the BB budget. This would lead to a shortage of BBs, and the BB could be redeemed at a premium—an appropriate reward for the newfound fiscal virtue. In short, if some part of our current troubles stem from the remarkable effectiveness of the professional leaning community, then we can only be helped by rewriting the rules so that they spend at least some of their time working on our behalf.

The main opponents to my plan, of course, will be the members of Congress who, with a few notable exceptions, don't really give a damn about the budget problems. This is because my proposal would undermine the current system that is used to reward local constituents for their political support. (When H.L. Mencken said elections are the advance auction of stolen goods, he wasn't whistling Dixie.) The current system spreads the costs of excessive spending around to all of us in the form of higher prices on the things we buy and higher payments on our mortgages, which in a way makes it difficult to trace the blame back to the actions of specific members of Congress. In contrast, my proposal concentrates those costs and imposes them on those standing in line for government money.

A side benefit would be to make companies re-evaluate the desirability of doing business with the government, rather than with private citizens, due to the risks of being paid in budget bucks. And the same goes for those who are looking for a job—jobs in private firms would look that much more attractive compared with government jobs. All in all, I can't see this as a drawback; those who found the BB exchange risk too much to bear could simply leave their government jobs and look for work in the private sector. And besides, I'm sure that before long someone would introduce a BB futures contract at the Board of Trade and the BB risk could be hedged in any case.

The idea, of course, is much too simple and effective ever to make it through Congress. But before you dismiss it out of hand, ask yourself what would happen to interest rates, commodity prices, and the dollar if my plan were adopted and the federal government could never again borrow a single dollar.

# 5

# Private Equity

I n 1986, my friend Nevin Hulsey arranged for me to speak about the economy at a conference in Palm Springs. Nevin is a terrific operating manager who had led the successful leveraged buyout of Kilsby Roberts, the country's leading metal tubing distributor, from Fluor Corp, a large, publicly traded engineering and construction company in Southern California that had been our client at CEI for many years. The conference was the annual meeting of Kelso & Company, the private equity firm that had financed the LBO and was the controlling owner of Kilsby Roberts.

That was the night I met Joe Schuchert, Kelso's legendary chairman and CEO. I discussed with him the impact of disinflation on asset markets and company performance, and described what our clients were doing to restructure their companies and improve the way they manage capital. After the dinner, Joe invited me to spend a week out of each month at Kelso's office in New York, learning about their portfolio companies and advising the CEOs on business strategy. How could I turn down an offer to learn about private equity from the company that had invented the industry?

At Kelso, I had the opportunity to learn about the capital markets where companies are bought and sold, about how to control capital spending and about governance. Joe, Frank Nickell (Nick) and their partners gave me the opportunity to invest in their deals—my in-

*Joe Schuchert, with me and Pamela in the late 1980s*

auguration into the joys of risk and return. Fortunately for me, Kelso's partners, in addition to being great friends, are extraordinary investors with an uncanny ability to choose managers and value companies.

But my carefree days as an investment voyeur and shareholder value mechanic soon came to an end. My friend Charlie Parker, who was chief investment officer of Continental Insurance, decided that the work I was doing with Kelso gave us a stream of interesting investment opportunities. With Charlie's help in securing Continental's backing, I was able to form Rutledge Capital in 1991—my first private equity fund.

## Rutledge Capital

During the 1990s, we made dozens of private equity investments at Rutledge Capital. In the beginning, we learned to shave on Kelso's beard by making follow-on investments, providing expansion capital for a number of Kelso's operating companies, and as a co-investor with other private equity groups. Later, we led a dozen middle-market LBOs of our own.

At Rutledge Capital, Jerry St. Dennis, Rob Tucker and I, along with the rest of our team, reviewed more than 100 business plans each month. We negotiated, financed and closed the purchases and sales of companies. We chaired boards of directors and worked with managers to build and execute business plans. We worked through all of the issues that fill every business owner's day—manufacturing, unions, hiring, firing, employment agreements, stock options, bonus plans, capital budgets, new products, foreign subsidiaries, trade shows, competitors, acquisitions, divestitures, vendors, insurance, regulations, patents, class action lawsuits, bank agreements, working capital lines and meeting payroll.

We had great victories and painful defeats. We worked very hard, and I got to work with my brother Tom every day. After two funds and more than thirty investments, however, we decided not to raise a third fund. I needed to take time off to help my dad work through his cancer treatments. We had portfolio companies that needed our attention. And I had decided that being a tough guy as Chairman of the Board was perhaps not the highest and best use of my talents. But I learned a ton about

being a business owner. My partners and colleagues are all now pursuing successful private equity careers. I have returned to my true love—traveling the world, learning about new ideas and helping start new ventures.

*Reviewing deals at Rutledge Capital with Jerry St. Dennis and Rob Tucker*

During the 15 years that we were making investments and growing companies at Rutledge Capital, I wrote the "Business Strategy" column for *Forbes* magazine, as well as hundreds of articles in newspapers and magazines, about owning a business and managing capital.

In this chapter, I want to share with you some of the ideas I learned during this period. They are just as valuable for a stock market investor as they are for a private equity investor. They are all based on one simple idea: when you buy a stock, you are not just buying a piece of paper—you are buying a piece of a business, with all the profits and losses, problems and opportunities that come along with being a business owner. The only way I know how to be a successful stock market investor is to do the same work you would do if you owned the business. Here are a few of those ideas.

## It Takes Time to Change a Business

Nothing is more dangerous than a man who believes he is always right. Over the course of their careers, managers learn which strategies work and which ones don't work through trial and error. They become very attached to these ideas, and have a hard time changing their ways when external conditions change. In the 1970s, for example, people learned to adopt business practices and investment strategies that fit an inflationary environment. The high-inflation 1970s served as training ground for the people who became the CEOs that were running our companies and managing the big investment portfolios when inflation turned south in 1981. In fact, many of these CEOs earned their positions because they did especially well in managing a company during high inflation. They had no idea what to do. For them, sudden disinflation and falling oil prices meant being thrust into a world turned upside down.

The same is true today, of course, but in reverse. The CEOs who earned their jobs by restructuring and tightening operations during the disinflationary 1980s and 1990s now have to figure out how to run a business in a world dominated by rapidly growing emerging economies and rising commodity prices.

Imagine you are a CEO who committed your company to a $500 million investment project two years ago, when oil prices were $30 per barrel. Today, two years later, $300 million of the project's funds have already been spent. Suddenly, you find that oil prices have jumped above $100 per barrel, and that everyone expects them to stay there. Worse yet, the 20% revenue increases that were used to justify the original profit projection have dried up, leaving a gap between the cash needs of the project and the internal funds that can be generated by the company. You, the CEO, have a real problem. What should you do?

As CEO in this situation, you must choose between two very unpleasant alternatives. You can either kill the project now and tell the board of directors that you just threw away $300 million, or you can decide to keep funding the project, borrowing to fill in the cash flow deficiency, perhaps digging a deeper grave for yourself in the process, in hopes that prices will turn around. Faced with such unpleasant alternatives, many CEOs choose to delay their final decision on killing the project.

Why do CEOs and investors delay such necessary structural adjustments? The answer may not be very scientific, but it is very human. They do not know for sure what future conditions will be like. And when in trouble, most people take refuge in the things that worked before. That's why it so often takes a change of managers to make an abrupt change in a business. Of course, that requires the members of the board of directors to make a decision too, which is no easier for the same reasons.

## Don't Let the CEO be Chairman Too

One of the lessons I learned in private equity is that the Chairman of the Board and the CEO should never be the same person. They have two very different jobs to do. It is the friendly tension between them that makes a business successful.

In 1989, when Deborah Allen and I wrote *Rust to Riches*, Japanese investors had just purchased Rockefeller Center and it seemed that everyone in the U.S. was convinced that Japan Inc. was going to take over America. We pointed out that although Japanese investors now owned Rockefeller Center, we still got to use it because it was too heavy for them to take home. We believed that stories about the imminent death of the U.S. economy were overstated. A decade of restructuring had made American companies more competitive than ever. In the opening chapter, we told the story of a company that forgot that lesson.

—

"On Monday we will discuss the case of General Motors," Professor Marshall told his strategic management class. As you know, we study cases to learn by identifying the mistakes of real managers in actual business situations. GM is the perfect case to study, because nowhere in the history of business have so many errors been committed by one group of managers. Destroying the largest and most powerful company in the world took a lot of work, but somehow GM's managers pulled it off.

"I want everyone to read *Concept of the Corporation*, Peter Drucker's classic analysis of the problems encountered in managing a large organization such as General Motors. And you might also like to read *Call Me Roger*, a very revealing book that details the role of Roger Smith, GM's chairman during the 1980s, in accelerating GM's demise. On Monday we'll ask two questions: 1)What cause the downfall of General Motors? 2) If you had taken over as GM's CEO in 1981, instead of Roger Smith, what would you have done to turn the company around and steer it into the twenty-first century?"

"General who?" asked a student sitting in the back row.

"I'm sorry, Rick," answered Professor Marshall. "Maybe it is asking a lot to expect students to know much about a company that went out of business twenty years before they were born. General Motors made cars, lots of them, back in the twentieth century. In fact, for a time between the end of World War II and the late 1980s GM was the largest corporation in the world. General Motors was the country's largest private employer, and accounted, either directly or indirectly through her dealers and suppliers, for more than 2 million jobs. In its heyday, GM had revenues of more than $100 billion per year, manufactured more than 60 percent of all cars sold in America, and was the largest auto maker in the world, bigger than Toyota, Honda, and Hyundai put together."

"If they were so powerful, then why haven't we ever heard of them?" asked Rick. "Why aren't they still making cars?"

"For the same reason the dinosaurs aren't walking down Main Street, Rick. They became extinct. General Motors went out of business more than thirty years ago. GM had so many layers of managers that it wasn't able to adapt to a rapidly changing global economy. They were too big, too slow, and too unresponsive to their customers. When oil prices jumped in the 1970s, GM was unable to produce the small, fuel-efficient cars their customers wanted, which allowed foreign companies like Toyota to establish a foothold in the U.S. market. Later, when imports started eating into GM's market share, GM whined for government protection rather than getting down to work. But their market share continued to decline.

"But it wasn't the imports that killed General Motors. Like all great empires, it died from within. GM's early success was the result of a management system forged by Alfred Sloan, an engineer brought in by Pierre du Pont to serve as GM's president and chief executive officer in 1923. Du Pont, as GM's largest shareholder, had been forced to take over the reins as CEO himself when GM's founder, Bill Durant, drove the company into the hands of its bankers for the second time in 1920. During Sloan's twenty-six-year tenure as GMs president and CEO, he developed and refined a system of decentralized management that was copied by companies all over the world. In his memoirs, *My Years with General Motors*, Sloan wrote, '...good management rests on a reconciliations of centralization and decentralization, or decentralization with coordinated control. Each of the conflicting elements in this concept has its unique re-sults in the operation of a business. From decentralization we get initiative, responsibility, development of personnel, decision close to the facts, flexibility—in short, all the qualities necessary for an organization to adapt to new conditions. From coordination we get efficiencies and economies.'

"Sloan's system led to GM's tradition of dividing executive power between a Chairman of the board, who was strictly a finance man who controlled the purse strings at the board level, and a strong president, typically an engineer by training, who served as chief ex-ecutive and ran the operations of the company. Sloan understood that engineers should build the cars and bean counters should con-trol the money. But it didn't take long after Sloan's departure for his lieutenants to screw it up. Two years after Sloan stepped down as chairman, Frederick Donner became the first finance man to be appointed as chairman and CEO since the days of Pierre du Pont. That was the beginning of the end for General Motors. GM lost its ability to adapt to change. Once the bean counters seized power, they never gave back the keys.

"Then, in 1981, the GM board appointed Roger Smith as chairman and CEO. They thought they were hiring a traditional finance guy who would cut costs and manage assets. What they got, instead, was a frustrated inventor who, just like Billy Durant back in the 1920s, liked to buy companies. Smith was quoted as saying, 'It's frustrating that we just can't spend the money sometimes as fast as we would like.' In the first half of the 1980s, GM spent $45 billion on new acquisitions and capital equipment but their break-even level of output went up by 30 percent! Smith once told a press conference back in the 1980s, 'I'm done sweating the details. Now I'm ready to move on to the twenty-first century.' Well here we are in the twenty-first century. But where is General Motors? Maybe they should have sweated a few more details after all." [...]

Economic change is not new. Peter Drucker, in *Innovation and Entrepreneurship*, reminds us that business managers have had to deal with changing business conditions as far back as we have records. And the most successful managers and investors are those who are able to identify, respond to, and exploit change, which Drucker calls entrepreneurial management. [...]

You can't protect a business against all possible risks. You must choose the one or two that you think are worth paying the costs to protect against.

## A Stock is Like a Bond

Forget price/earnings, price/book and price/cash flow ratios. Valuing businesses for private equity investment, I learned that cash flow and intrinsic value are much better measures of investment value.

Warren Buffett, like Benjamin Graham and John Burr Williams before him, has suggested that the right way to think about the value of a business is to view it as a bond where investors receive a variable stream of coupons. These coupons take the form of dividend payments or share repurchases as the company produces cash flow in excess of the incremental capital it needs to run and grow its business.

That's how a long-term bond is priced: its value is the discounted present value of all the payments investors expect to receive over the bond's life, including coupons and the return of principal that investors will get when the bond matures.

Private equity investors value a business in the same way. The value of a business is the present value of its expected free cash flow to investors. With a business, however, there is no repayment of principal in ten, or twenty, or thirty years, so an investor must estimate profits far into the future. It takes a good understanding of the business, its markets and its prospects to do this.

This view flies in the face of the perceived wisdom that the stock market is obsessed with short-term performance. In fact, the stock market must take an even longer-term view than the bond market for the simple reason that a company's equity coupons go on, in principle, forever, while even a long-term government bond's principal will be repaid in only 30 years.

Paul Davis and Deborah Allen, my colleagues at Rutledge Research, and I developed a model that calculates the intrinsic value of the S&P 500. We used analysts' estimates for sales growth, profit margins and working capital needs, and current figures for long-term interest rates and the after-tax cost of equity capital. The present value of the resulting free cash flow is the intrinsic value of the overall stock market.

Even more interesting than the intrinsic value, however, is the cash flow profile of the S&P's future coupons. Only 2% of the intrinsic value of the S&P industrials is based on profits earned within the first year; i.e., the market's intrinsic value would decline by only 2% if its owners donated all first-year free cash flow to the Boy Scouts. The first ten future years together account for only one-fourth of total value. And you would have to reach more than 30 years into the future to account for half of the stock market's intrinsic value. Analytically, the market is a *very* long-term bond, which is why stock prices are so sensitive to changes in interest rates.

This shows why price/earnings, price/book value and price/cash flow ratios are unreliable measures of valuation. None capture the essential forward-looking nature of investing in the stock market or owning a business.

Complex though it may sound, this way of looking at stocks is valuable for long-term investors. It is equally valuable for chief executives in developing business strategies to deliver sustainable value to their shareholders.

Managers at one extremely profitable and fast-growing company I know were surprised to learn that the duration—or time-weighted average maturity—of cash flows implied by the market's valuation of their company's stock was less than 14 years, compared with 36 years for the S&P. Investors were not giving the company credit for being able to sustain its recent performance into the future.

This company's problem was not growth or profitability, but whether investors believed that the performance was sustainable. One way to create sustainable value is to become the low-cost producer. Another way is to develop branded products that customers will value more highly than competitive commodity products. Both strategies will lead to higher sustainable operating margins, improved market share and a higher stock price.

Investors should ask the same questions about the stocks they own. Does the company have a defendable franchise for creating shareholder value, i.e., does it have the ability to produce sustainable returns for shareholders in excess of those that entrants could earn? Are its managers doing the things today that are necessary to develop and protect those advantages in the future?

## Intrinsic Value Investing

When we say intrinsic value, we mean it. To us, it means valuing an investment based strictly on estimates of its future free cash flow stream and the investor's after-tax cost of capital, just as if the market were closed and that investor were going to own the investment forever. It means basing those estimates on complete sets of projected financial statements for the life of the business, the same way private equity investors value an enterprise. And it means doing the work to understand the market forces that determine the revenues, costs, profit margins, capital intensity, capital structure and interest rates that ultimately drive the evolution of cash flow.

## Value Drivers

Value drivers are the things you have to input in order to build a model that projects a company's future financial statements. They include sales growth rates, cost of goods sold margins, SG&A expense ratios, tax rates, capital spending rates, depreciation rates, working capital, fixed assets per dollar of sales, interest costs and capital structure, among other variables.

We specify value driver paths for each year during a thirty-year forecast period and build a complete set of financial statements (Profit and Loss, Balance Sheet and Statement of Cash Flows) for thirty years into the future. The present value of the free cash flow estimates from these statements gives us the intrinsic value of the enterprise. Finally, we subtract debt and divide by shares to get the intrinsic value of equity per share.

## The Shoebox Never Lies

It is always important to read financial statements with your skeptical spectacles on. They are a terrible measure of the health of a company, even in the best of circumstances. Earnings are always a judgment call; which outlays to capitalize, which to expense, when to recognize revenues and how to value assets are never black and white.

Accounting is a blunt instrument, not well-suited for today's companies. Balance sheets were invented to keep track of the liquidation value of a business, which is why we record the only interesting part of the balance sheet—the difference between the value of a business and the value of its assets—as goodwill. The only part of a business that we really understand is its cash flow. The shoebox never lies.

Unfortunately, future cash flow, the true basis of value, is extremely difficult to predict, even for insiders. And it always will be.

## Value Investors Never Have Fun

Value investing is a lonely business. You have to have a view of the value of assets at all times, but you rarely get to do anything because the markets price assets more or less fairly most of the time. When markets are booming and everybody else is excited about the future, as they were in 1999, you sell your stocks and leave the party before you have even had cocktails. Then, when stocks get cheap again, as they did in 2003, and everybody is saying that only a fool would be in the market, you buy again. Nobody likes a value investor. Value investors never have any fun.

They do, however, make money. Stock prices can wander quite far from intrinsic value for many months at a time, but they eventually find their way home again. Investors who buy when prices fall well below intrinsic value—say 20%—and sell when prices climb well above intrinsic value make significant gains over long periods. Today is just such a period.

Today's panic has been largely caused by a sudden and dramatic loss of investor confidence in the U.S. economy, triggered by the sub-prime mortgage meltdown. But the mortgage meltdown was caused by a capital market problem—a blackout in the mortgage-backed securities market—not by a recession. Last summer, mortgage securities holders lost confidence in their ability to understand and predict the cash flow stream they would receive from these complicated securities. They simply backed away from the table for a while until the fog cleared; mortgage markets virtually stopped trading.

But security market blackouts do not last forever. Vulture investors are stepping in to buy troubled assets. When markets are again able to price securities, the market for new mortgages will be open for business again. I expect that to happen later this year. When it does, commentators will be surprised, but value investors who own shares in large-cap U.S. companies with branded products, growing cash profits and exposure to fast-growing Asia will be well rewarded for their patience.

## Risk is a Not Just a Four Letter Word

For four decades, students learned from their professors that risk means volatility. It can be measured by sigma ($\sigma$), the standard deviation of a stock price over some historical period, or by beta ($\beta$), its first cousin that measures how much a particular stock price rises and falls with re-spsect to the overall market. But when changes in fundamentals take place, in drivers such as sales growth, margins, risk and cost of capital, they blow backward-looking sigma estimates out of the water, destroying the capital invested using these estimates. Standard Wall Street practice when everything goes wrong is to call these episodes "six-sigma events." Translated into English, this means "Hey, things that are *that* improbable are never supposed to *actually* happen. This is not my fault." Unfortunately, giving the situation a fancy name doesn't bring back the money.

Sigma worship is pervasive on Wall Street. It is used in currency and mortgage hedging, asset allocation, credit risk management and options pricing. This dominance means that there is a tremendous opportunity waiting for anyone who can come up with a better mousetrap. We think intrinsic risk is that better mousetrap.

We view a security as a shopping bag filled with claims on future cash flows. Think of them as dated coupons representing the future profits, dividends, or free cash flows of companies, agencies, or governments. A securities market is just a place where you take the particular bag that you own to sell it to someone else for cash today. Think of it as an eBay for bags of paper IOUs.

There are two different ways you can leave the market with empty pockets: these are the two types of financial risk. The first type of risk is the worry that you will get to the market with your bag brimming over with future cash flows, but there is nobody there willing to pay you a fair price for it. We will call the risk that nobody is home *market risk*. This is the risk that Efficient Market Theory, Modern Portfolio Theory, the Capital Asset Pricing Model (CAPM) and the Black-Scholes theorem all talk about. Market risk can be very important when you are forced to sell things quickly or at the wrong time (like today). Given plenty of time to wait, however, market risk is not a big deal, especially in markets as deep and liquid as the U.S. capital markets.

The second type of risk is much more important. It is the worry that you will bring your bag of future cash flow claims to the market and find plenty of buyers, but nobody will pay you for it because when they look inside the bag, it is empty. Unfortunately, the fair price for an empty bag is zero, even in an efficient market. Unlike market risk, waiting won't help. Empty bag risk, or *intrinsic risk*, is the one risk that matters for long-term investors, because it can make even patient, liquid investors lose all of their capital.

One reason for the popularity of sigma, beta, and covariance estimates as proxies for market risk is that they are so easy to produce. Anyone with a laptop computer, a spreadsheet and a copy of *Barron's* can crank out estimates by the truckload in the time it takes to drink a vanilla latte.

Estimating intrinsic risk takes more work. To measure the intrinsic risk of a security, you must understand all of the factors, or value drivers, that will determine its future cash flows, such as sales growth, profit margins and cost of capital. You must make judgments about the likely path of each driver for many years into the future. And you must know the likelihood that your value driver estimates will be wrong. This work requires intimate knowledge of a company, its markets, and the economy. This is the work that a good security analyst or credit analyst does every day. It is very hard to do.

We believe this work is necessary in order to understand, measure and manage intrinsic risk. If you are not able to build a complete set of financial statements for a company for many years into the future, the same way a private equity investor does when buying a controlling interest in a business, you do not understand the intrinsic risk of its cash flows.

The complete list of value drivers for a company includes all of the inputs you would have to know to generate its financial statements. They can be grouped into categories driving revenues (units sold, product price, growth rates), margins (costs and productivity), capital turnover (inventory, receivables, capital spending), cost of capital, capital structure (leverage) and taxes.

Each driver has an uncertain future path that is a source of intrinsic risk to the company. Sales growth, for example, depends on the growth rate of the economy, inflation, industry structure and technology. In principle, each driver can be represented by a set of probability distributions for each future period, each one looking a lot like the one used in finance books to represent a firm. Estimates of the means, standard deviations and other parameters of these distributions can be used to generate estimates of intrinsic value and intrinsic risk for companies in the stock market by pushing them through standard private equity spreadsheet math. The result is a set of distributions of free cash flow for future periods.

We have estimated the intrinsic value of hundreds of companies in dozens of industries over the past ten years, in different growth and interest rate environments. Based upon our work, three drivers dominate the action. If you get sales growth, profit margins and cost of capital right, the rest don't matter.

We determine the risk attributable to changes in these drivers by conducting a sensitivity analysis on the company's future cash flow and, therefore, on intrinsic value. First we estimate intrinsic value assuming the most likely path of the drivers over the forecast period, i.e., using the means of the future driver distributions. Next, we measure the effect on intrinsic value of varying the drivers by the amount of likely uncertainty around its assumed level. We do this for each driver, for every company, for every industry.

Several patterns emerge from this work. First, the intrinsic value sensitivities are highly dependent on initial driver levels. At today's low interest rates, for example, sensitivities to changes in cost of capital—long-term interest rates—are huge. A one percentage point drop in the weighted average cost of capital today would increase intrinsic value by more than 25%. That makes interest rates extremely important for intrinsic risk, not just for financial companies, but for all companies in the stock market.

Quantitative types will recognize this as an estimate of duration (roughly the number of years into the future you have to go before the present value of the expected cash flow adds up to more than half of the firm's intrinsic value), and will know that duration increases as interest rates fall. Our estimates show that equity durations, and therefore cost of capital sensitivities, are generally much larger than the duration of even the longest term bonds. This makes logical sense because bonds mature while equities, in principle, go on forever, and because bond coupons are flat over time while free cash flow grows (at least in the projections) for equities. This makes understanding interest rates very important for all equity investors.

Second, sensitivities differ markedly across industries and companies, even in the same economic environment, because different industries will have different time shapes for future cash flows. For example, a fast-growing tech start-up, with its best cash flows many years away will have a higher duration and interest sensitivity than a mature company with declining sales.

This gives diversification a new meaning. Holding a large number of stocks in a portfolio does not effectively diversify intrinsic risk. Diversification of intrinsic risk means explicitly managing the acceptable exposure to the risk contributed by each driver, i.e., not betting all your eggs on one driver.

Intrinsic risk can help an investor set a steady course during turbulent market periods such as we are experiencing today. Traditional risk measures would tell us that the increased volatility that followed the mortgage crisis means that stocks have become riskier investments. The intrinsic value approach, in contrast, asks whether the meltdown has produced any long-lasting changes in the outlook for value drivers. If not, as we believe is the case for most industries today, then current prices offer tremendous value for investors.

## Intellectual Capital Accounting

"You've GOT to be kidding!" I told the voice on the phone. I had gotten a call at dinnertime telling me my credit line would be cut off if I didn't make a payment the next day. "Do you know how rich I am? I may not have any money, but I am…an intellectual capital tycoon! I have a doctorate in economics and a Phi Beta Kappa key. My wife studied psychopharmacology, plays the flute, and speaks French. And on our family balance sheet my five children have already capitalized one Ph.D., two masters degrees, five bachelor's degrees, five prep school degrees, and two fancy East Coast private-grade-school honor-roll certificates. We have books all over the house and our own website. We recycle everything. We value diversity. My children have studied Latin, for crissake. And with all this intellectual capital, you want to cut off my credit card?"

This argument, or some variant of it, is the mantra of knowledge workers, knowledge consultants, chief knowledge officers and New Age knowledge accountants who have figured out there are big bucks to be made in intellectual capital, or IC to those in the know. Like professors everywhere, they argue it is time for society to recognize the value of people who are smart rather than those who create profits. They want every company in America to have an IC strategy, which they will help you create and implement for a fee.

After reading the academic papers in the field, I have formalized a strategy that I can recommend without reservation: If you meet people who have the word knowledge anywhere on their business card, don't give them any money! Just put the card down and back away slowly. At best, IC will bore you to death. At worst, IC is a potential Trojan horse for those who want stakeholders, not shareholders, to control our companies. It is time to drive a stake through the heart of this movement now, before any real damage is done.

The most troubling idea of the IC mavens is to tinker with financial statements, so companies full of smart people who don't make profits look more attractive to investors. Some want to include the capitalized value of workers' ideas on the balance sheet. Some want to include cultural factors, such as the gender composition of the workforce, as if it is somehow a driver of the profitability of a company. And some want to use measurements of intellectual capital to influence the credit markets or public policy. But there is a big difference between smart and effective; I'll take an effective person over a smart one any day.

Monkeying with financial statements, for almost any reason, is a terrible idea. Investors have 500 years of practice interpreting financial statements while learning to understand, project, get comfortable with and value our roughly $200 trillion in total assets. In doing so, they have developed methods to adjust for many of the anomalies (for example, amortization of goodwill, which can only be defined by describing what it is not) that emerge from our archaic double-entry bookkeeping practices from time to time. Scrambling the financial data we use to make such judgments would render these methods less useful. It also would throw up a cloud of uncertainty that would make assets more risky, and therefore less valuable. Giving people more information is fine: they can make their own judgments. Tinkering with the balance sheet is not a good idea.

Although intellectual capital is important, it should be left off the balance sheet. Balance sheets are for stuff, not people or ideas. People aren't assets because you can't own them, at least not in this country; you can only rent them (I'm abstracting from alimony here). Ideas are not assets either because you can't keep them bottled up for very long (except for the secret formula for Coke). If you want to measure the value of people and their ideas, you need to look at cash flows, not assets. Balance sheets measure the value of things you own; cash flows measure the value of things you rent.

IC evangelists claim that knowledge is accelerating at such an incredible rate that our brains are going to explode. (Stand back, I'm getting smarter.) They also claim that financial measures have become useless and obsolete because the value of intellectual capital is swamping everything in determining the value of today's companies. Don't believe them on either count.

Their first point is naïve, as Daniel Boorstin details in his fabulous books, *The Discoverers* and *The Creators*. There have always been very smart people who have worked hard to learn as much as they could during their lifetimes. I am confident that Leonardo da Vinci and Isaac Newton would be able to compete today—even in Silicon Valley.

Nor is the speed at which information flows a new phenomenon. Sir Arthur Conan Doyle wrote about the five daily mail deliveries in London in the 19th century, not to mention the telegraph and Holmes' real-time messenger boys—human precursors to the Internet. Short travel distances between cultural hubs (Florence, Vienna, Paris, London) and competition among royal patrons for the talents of creative people led to a great deal of interaction among artists, writers, scientists, and inventors since the time of the Renaissance. And the idea that intellectual capital has value is not new. In 1839, the French Academy of Sciences arranged for the French government to purchase Louis Daguerre's secret process for fixing an image on a plate of silver, or *daguerreotype*, in exchange for a lifetime annuity for the inventor, and then gave the idea to the public at no cost. Photography quickly spread across Europe.

The second point, that IC is becoming so valuable that it renders balance sheets obsolete as a measure of a company's value, is irrelevant. Balance sheets were never intended to measure the value of a company, and they are not used for that purpose by serious investors. At best, balance sheets give an investor a rough idea of the value that can be realized by killing a company, breaking it up and selling it in pieces—and then only after careful scrutiny. It's like saying the value of a human being is $2.89, because that's all the component chemicals in our body would fetch in the marketplace. The value of a business as a going concern is determined by its cash flows or profits, not by its assets.

The real question posed by intellectual capital is not one of measurement or financial reporting; it is how to manage the companies. To the extent that today's technology companies derive their value in the capital markets from distant income streams that depend on a continual introduction of new products created by a large group of very smart people, managers must deal with a serious sustainability question. How are they going to hold the people together long enough to accomplish their objectives? Since they can't own the "assets"—the people who think up the ideas—the next best thing is to have the people own the income streams created by their own efforts. In technology companies, broad and deep employee stock ownership is extremely important.

With that in mind, we should ask ourselves what an investor should know about a company's IC before investing in the company. At the top of my list would be information about the long-term incentives of the people who run the organization. I'd want to make sure that more than half their total pay was determined (both up and down) by performance, and that managers were at risk in the company's stock. It may take a village to raise a child, but it takes an owner, not a salaryman, to build a company.

# 6

# Thermo-Economics

T his chapter is based upon a framework for thinking about economic growth, trade, capital flows and questions of economic and
financial instability that I have been developing at the Chinese Academy of Sciences. In this framework, drawn from the natural sciences,
economic activity is viewed as transformations of solar energy—both
*current* solar energy and *vintage* solar energy, stored in the form of natural
resources, human capital, physical capital and technology—driven by the
laws of thermodynamics.

This chapter explains why efficient global capital markets and
high-speed communications networks have accelerated global economic
growth. It then discusses recent developments in non-equilibrium thermodynamics (NET) to outline how rapid growth, accelerating trade and
cross-country capital flows are linked to turbulence, in the form of protectionism and social and political instability. It discusses policies for mit-

igating the harmful impact of unavoidable turbulence and protectionism on growth. Finally, it discusses the implications of this framework for the question of energy security.

## Global Growth

At Nobelist Robert Mundell's Santa Columba Conference in the summer of 2007, the assembled group of specialists in international finance agreed on two points: 1) the global economy is growing as fast as it has at any time in recorded history, led by the spectacular reform-driven performances of China and India, and 2) the greatest risk to sustained global growth is political backlash and rising protectionism, especially in the United States.

Advances in information technology and communications networks have driven recent increases in global growth through three primary channels.

First, they have made it possible for people to view each other's lives on their televisions—in real time—for the first time in history. This has exposed gaping income and wealth differentials across nations, and has motivated people in low-income countries to demand pro-growth policy reforms from their governments.

Second, communications technology has made it easier, faster, and cheaper to move resources around the globe to take advantage of price and return differentials. Labor, capital and technology now move at the speed of light through fiber-optic networks at low cost, which has accelerated growth in emerging economies.

Third, advances in global capital markets since the early 1980s have reduced the cost of moving capital and, therefore, the minimum return-differential threshold for triggering capital redeployment.[1] Policy reforms, including last year's WTO-mandated opening of China's capital markets, have made capital easier still to move. The result has been broader and deeper capital markets, faster adjustment and higher economic growth.

These changes have increased global growth, profits and stock market values; they have also created growing economic and political conflicts within and among nations. These conflicts are manifesting themselves as rising protectionist pressures around the world.[2]

In two recent papers (Rutledge 2007a, 2007b), I have outlined a new framework for analyzing economic activity based on the laws of thermodynamics, which describes the energy transfers that drive all activity on earth—including economic activity. In this framework, entrepreneurs respond to energy gradients (price and return differentials) by employing both current solar energy and stored solar energy—in the form of natural resources, human capital, physical capital, and technology—to create work, or economic activity. Resource flows within and between nations are driven by price and return gradients according to

---

[1]    Arrhenius Behavior states that the rate of a chemical reaction increases with rising temperature (Atkins (1991), pages 104-105). First proposed by the Dutch chemist Jacobus van't Hoff (1884) and interpreted by Svante Arrhenius in 1889, the rule states that reaction rate is an exponential function of temperature, or Rate = $k_0 e^{-Ta/T}$. In this expression, $T_a$ represents the reaction-specific activation temperature—the threshold below which no reaction will occur. Ludwig Boltzmann derived a related expression for the proportion of collisions between molecules in a reaction that occurs with at least the activation energy $E_a$ (the threshold below which no reaction will occur) as $e^{-Ea/kT}$, where k, known as Boltzmann's constant, is a fundamental constant of nature. The economic interpretation of $E_a$ is the minimum price difference, in microeconomics, or minimum return on capital difference, in capital markets, required to trigger a profitable arbitrage transaction. $E_a$ represents the friction, transportation costs, or transactions costs of engaging in markets. Reducing $E_a$ increases adjustment speed for a given price differential, also known as a price *gradient*.

[2]    Recent U.S. examples include the aborted attempt of China's CNOOC to acquire Unocal and the failed Dubai Ports purchase—both killed by political backlash in the U.S. Congress—the recent action against the Chinese paper industry by the U.S. Commerce Department, the Schumer-Graham legislation under discussion in Congress and the aborted attempt of China's Huawei to make a minority investment in 3Com.

the second law of thermodynamics.[3] Policies impact resource flows by steepening or flattening price and return gradients, providing incentives, or signals, for entrepreneurs to change their behavior.

This framework allows us to draw on recent important developments in non-equilibrium thermodynamics (NET),[4] pioneered by Ilya Prigogine, that can help us understand the dynamic behavior of systems, including economic systems, over time. NET sheds light on questions of so-called market failures, including recessions, asset market bubbles and trade wars.

I will summarize this framework below. In the next section, we will describe the link between thermodynamics and economic activity.

## Thermodynamics Framework of Economic Activity

To Democritus, writing 2,500 years ago, the universe was comprised of "atoms and a void."[5] To a modern physicist, there is only matter and energy. In fact, as Einstein (1905) showed in his famous equation $E=mc^2$, matter and energy are conceptually interchangeable. In this view, all activity on earth can be viewed as energy transformations driven by the flow of energy from the sun.[6]

Mining solar energy to produce usable products, the subject of physics and engineering, is the domain of thermodynamics. Richard Feynman (1989) explains:

---

[3] The second law of thermodynamics states that matter and energy have a tendency to disperse to a less orderly form, or in Clausius's words, "heat cannot by itself pass from a colder to a warmer body" (Kondepudi (1998), page 84). The second law was established by Sadi Carnot in 1824, Rudolph Clausius in 1850 and Lord Kelvin in 1851, and was applied to chemical reactions by Josiah Gibbs in the 1870s. Economists will recognize Josiah Gibbs's most famous student—Irving Fisher.

[4] For a review of recent writings in NET, see Schneider and Sagan (2005) and Prigogine (1997).

[5] "According to convention, there is fire, there is water, there is air, and there is earth. There is a sweet and a bitter, and a hot and a cold. According to convention there is inherent order in the universe. In truth, there is only atoms and a void" (Democritus, 400 B.C., quoted in Dressler and Potter (1991) page 1).

[6] Stated by Boltzmann (1886), page 24, as quoted in Schneider and Sagan (2005).

There is a fact, or if you wish, a law, governing all natural phenomena that are known to date. There is no known exception to this law—it is exact as far as we know. The law is called the conservation of energy. It states that there is a certain quantity, which we call energy, that does not change in the manifold changes which nature undergoes. That is a most abstract idea, because it is a mathematical principle; it says that there is a numerical quantity, which does not change when something happens. It is not a description of a mechanism, or anything concrete; it is just a strange fact that we can calculate some number and when we finish watching nature go through her tricks and calculate the number again, it is the same. (page 4.1)

[...] Energy has a large number of forms...gravitational energy, kinetic energy, heat energy, elastic energy, electrical energy, chemical energy, radiant energy, nuclear energy, mass energy. ...it is important to realize that in physics today, we have no knowledge of what energy is. (page 4.2)

[...] Although we know for a fact that energy is conserved, the energy available for human utility is not conserved so easily. The laws that govern how much energy is available are called the laws of thermodynamics and involve a concept called entropy for irreversible thermodynamic processes. (page 4.8)

[...] Finally, we must remark on the question of where we can get our supplies of energy today. Our supplies of energy are the sun, rain, coal, uranium, and hydrogen. The sun makes the rain and coal also, so that all these are from the sun. Although energy is conserved, nature does not seem to be interested in it; she liberates a lot of energy from the sun, but only one part in two billion falls on the earth. Nature has conservation of energy, but does not really care; she spends a lot of it in all directions. We have already obtained energy from uranium; we can also get energy from hydrogen, but at present only in an explosive and dangerous condition. If it can be controlled in thermonuclear reactions, it turns out that the energy that can be obtained from 10 quarts of water per second is equal to all of the electrical power generated in the United States. With 150 gallons of running water a minute, you have enough fuel to supply all the energy that is used in the United States today! Therefore it is up to the physicist to figure out how to liberate us from the need for having energy. It can be done. (page 4.8)

## Work, Coherent Energy and Economic Activity

I used to teach macroeconomics with a straight face. This section is not intended to modify macroeconomics, however; it is intended to completely replace it with a framework that makes more sense. Macro-economists, of course, won't like that. Orthodox macroeconomics, developed following last century's Great Depression, is obsessed with analyzing who is spending money—consumers, businesses, the government, or foreigners. More recently, supply-side economics, pioneered by 1999 Nobel-winner Robert Mundell, has focused attention on the resources available for production and on the incentives for people to use their energies toward utilizing resources productively. As Feynman pointed out, to a physicist, there is only one resource that drives all activity on earth—the energy from the sun.

The purpose of macroeconomics is to measure and explain variations in economic activity—how much work the people in an economy perform during a given time period. Work creates wealth and generates incomes. Work earns paychecks; work generates profits. Economists refer to total economic activity as Gross Domestic Product (GDP). It would be more useful to think of total economic activity as Gross National Work (GNW).

Physicists have been measuring work since Galileo rolled a ball down an incline 500 years ago. To a physicist, work is a result of energy transformation.

### Figure 5: Work vs. Heat

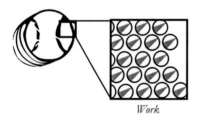

*Work*

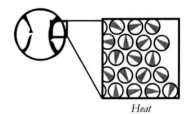

*Heat*

To illustrate, think of the baseballs in Figure 5. The baseball on the left has been thrown by a major league pitcher; every particle in the ball is moving at 97 miles per hour towards the catcher's mitt. This orderly situation is an example of work, also known as kinetic energy, or coherent energy.

Every particle in the baseball on the right is also moving at 97 miles per hour; but the baseball, viewed as a macro object, or system of particles, is not visibly moving. In this case, we have set the particles in motion by heating the baseball to a high temperature—the particles are moving rapidly, but in random directions, colliding frequently with each other. This example of chaotic motion is called heat, thermal energy, or incoherent energy.

In economics, the picture on the left represents productive economic activity, where people are engaging in work to produce goods and services. The picture on the right represents cost, wasted effort, inefficiency, or conflict. The policy that encourages people to produce the largest possible value of work (coherent energy) and the smallest amount of heat (incoherent energy), given available resources, will result in the highest GDP and the highest living standard.

There is a law of conservation of energy stating that energy can be transformed but never created or destroyed. Unfortunately, as Feynman hinted, there is no law of conservation of work. Work can be destroyed by policies that blunt incentives or make it more difficult (require more energy) for people to create wealth. Subsidies, tariffs, quotas, price controls, excise taxes and burdensome or unpredictable regulations reduce work. Taxing an activity destroys work. A government should collect tax revenues in the manner that destroys the least amount of work. Taxing work by imposing taxes on income and profits destroys work and reduces GDP.

Excessive tax rates, subsidies to inefficient producers, trade restrictions and policies that encourage conflict between one group or class of people and another group are examples of bad policies; they create heat and destroy work. Good policies increase work. From this perspective, the proper target for monetary policy is the policy that results in the most productive work. That policy is zero real asset inflation, i.e., zero capital gains for the existing stock of tangible assets, into which no further work—energy—is being invested. This would focus investors' attention on the underlying cash flows of an investment and force wealth-creating energies into the security markets where they can finance new capital formation. For central bankers, it means following a price rule that would stabilize land, property and commodity prices. This was precisely the thinking that we brought to the Reagan economic team in 1981.

In markets, work is created when people respond to price and return differences that signal profitable opportunities to redeploy resources. In flow markets, we call it supply and demand; in asset markets, we call it portfolio balance. Both are simply restatements of the second law of thermodynamics. Arbitrage, fed by price and return differentials, is the only law we need to build a macroeconomic theory of work.

Arbitrage is not just a Wall Street activity—it's what we all do every day. We arbitrage gasoline prices between local gas stations by buying gas from the station with the lowest price. We arbitrage prices of bottles of shampoo at the grocery store. We arbitrage waiting times when we choose which line to stand in at the checkout counter. We arbitrage labor decisions, savings decisions, investment descisions and trade decisions, whether across town or across the world.

There is only one meaningful statement in all of economics: people arbitrage relative price differentials. And that idea—that people make choices to improve their wealth—is the essence of supply-side economics. Just as with thermodynamics, the power of supply-side analysis is derived from its simplicity and its universal applicability.

This suggests a litmus test for economic theories. If an analysis cannot be reduced to a description of people engaging in arbitrage activities, it is simply not economics. Unfortunately, macroeconomics as it is usually taught and practiced today—focusing on mechanical rules to predict people's expenditures—fails this test.

Trade—whether within a community or between nations—increases the aggregate amount of work and raises aggregate income, as economists have agreed upon since the time of David Ricardo. That is the reason that economists support free trade policy. Changes in trade patterns require changes in resource allocation that have important impacts on individuals. As we will see in a later section, these changes can lead to turbulence in the form of social instability and protectionism.

## Solar Energy Drives All Work

All activity on earth, including economic activity, is driven by the flow of energy from the sun. The second law of thermodynamics states that heat flows from warm to cold bodies. The difference between the 5,800K (5,800 degrees Kelvin) surface temperature of the sun and the 280K temperature of the earth's surface causes energy to flow from the sun to the earth in the form of radiation, producing work and heat on earth.

The sun is a giant thermonuclear reactor that has been turning five million tons of hydrogen into helium each second for five billion years. Its temperatures vary from 15 million K at its core to as low as 4,000K in sunspots. The rate of energy delivered to earth by the sun, 1.36 kilowatts (KW) per square meter, has long been referred to as the solar constant, although recent measurements show it varies by as much as 0.2%. (That 0.2% of variation equals four times all human energy consumed on earth today.) In all, only one billionth of total solar energy actually strikes the earth. But even this tiny fraction amounts to five million horsepower per square mile.

## Figure 6: Sun-Earth Flux

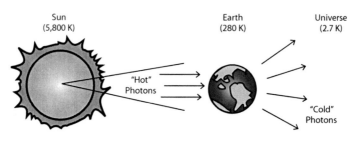

*(Schneider and Sagan, 2005)*

About two-thirds of the radiation that hits the earth's atmosphere strikes the earth's surface; the remaining third is absorbed by clouds as heat or reflected back into space. Only about 1% of energy striking the surface is converted into stored energy in organic molecules through photosynthesis. The energy stored in this way each year comes to about 1,018 kilojoules—approximately 30 times current global energy consumption (Atkins, page 210).

Through this seemingly wasteful collection process, stored sunlight makes the earth inhabitable. Sunlight trapped by photosynthesis produces the carbohydrates that the plants use to feed themselves (plants are autotrophes that produce their own food), which in turn provide the food for plant-eaters and animal-eaters (heterotrophes, species that do not produce their own food) such as humans.

Economic activity is the directed transformation and distribution of solar energy to satisfy the needs of man. We can think of stored solar energy as having a solar vintage, similar to the vintage marked on a bottle of wine. This vintage marks the year that the solar energy was captured in the form of organic molecules.

## Figure 7: Storing Solar Energy

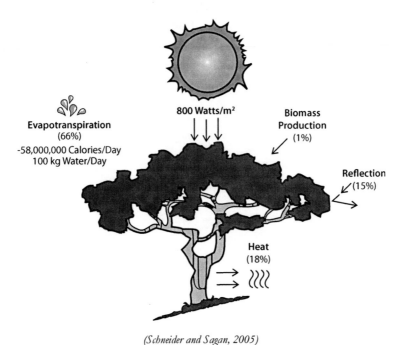

*(Schneider and Sagan, 2005)*

For most of human history, people earned a bare subsistence living as hunter-gatherers, harvesting current and recently stored solar energy in the form of living plants and animals. Hunter-gatherers harvested only very young solar vintages; for them the oldest vintage available was the wood they used for fuel, which had been stored only years or decades before.

Modern man enjoys a dramatically higher living standard than that of the hunter-gatherers because we have learned how to augment current solar energy by reaching deep into the wine cellar of vintage sunlight to mine energy stored in the distant past.

Wood has been man's primary fuel source for almost all of recorded history. Wood was only surpassed by coal in the closing decades of the nineteenth century, as shown in Figure 8. Wood energy has a solar vintage measured in decades. In contrast, the sunlight stored in the form of coal reached the earth 350 million years ago during the Carboniferous Period of the Later Paleozoic Era, when vast forests flourished in river deltas (Maiklen, page 269). Coal was succeeded first by oil, then by gas, after 1950. Together, fossil fuels provide about 85% of the energy we use today.

### Figure 8:  Stored Energy Consumption by Source, 1750-2005

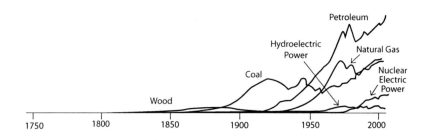

*(Energy Information Administration, 2006, page 2)*

But fossil fuels are only one form of stored energy; their consumption accounts for only a small percentage of GDP in most nations. The bulk of energy used to produce work is the energy stored as human capital (stored food energy, knowledge and experience), technology (stored knowledge), and tools (technology and knowledge stored as physical capital goods), as depicted in Figure 9. All are mechanisms for storing solar energy for a later time, when it can be used to generate work by making people's efforts more productive.

## Figure 9: Stored Energy Powers Work

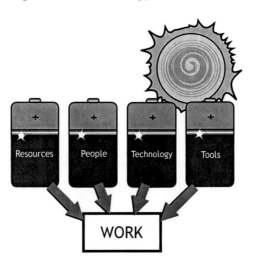

Wealth represents our command over stored energy. People use stored energy to produce work, which is valued in markets using prices that reflect relative scarcities. National income, or GDP, is a measure of Gross National Work, the price-weighted sum of all work.

## Arbitrage Drives the Global Economy

Stores of energy are not evenly distributed around the globe. Oil and gas are concentrated in the Arabian Gulf, with significant deposits in Russia, Africa, South America and Australia. Technology and physical capital are concentrated in North America, Western Europe and Japan. Human capital is concentrated in Asia.

If national economies are closed (without trade), then national endowments of stored energy determine relative prices, which vary from nation to nation. International trade theory refers to this closed system as autarky, illustrated in Figure 10 by two compartments of a washtub that are separated by a barrier.

### Figure 10: Closed Systems—Autarky

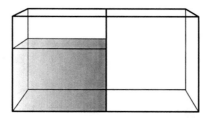

When two formerly closed systems are brought into communication to form a new single, open system, as in Figure 11, the second law of thermodynamics forces energy to disperse. In the washtub example, the pressure differential caused by different water levels forces water to flow from the full tank into the empty one. This adjustment also works for temperature changes between high and low pressure systems in meteorology as well as in chemical reactions. All are, formally, cooling processes in which a new open system moves toward a low energy state. In economics, this represents arbitrage behavior; entrepreneurs redeploy resources in response to price or return differentials.

### Figure 11: Open Systems—Arbitrage

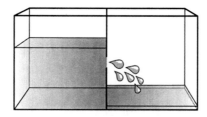

In the absence of continuing energy flows, the end result will be thermal equilibrium, illustrated in Figure 12, at which point no further net energy flow takes place. This is also known as the zeroth law of thermodynamics. In economics, a market is defined as an area in which prices tend to converge to a single level. This law of one price in economics corresponds to thermal equilibrium where no further net energy or resource flow will take place.

## Figure 12: Thermal Equilibrium—Law of One Price

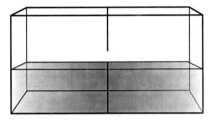

In today's connected global economy, stored energy imbalances lead to price and return differentials. This can trigger arbitrage activities in which entrepreneurs redeploy resources toward areas of greater relative scarcity. This can be viewed in two equivalent ways.

## Figure 13: Arbitrage—Physical Capital

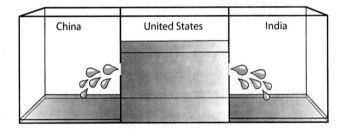

From the point of view of an owner of physical capital, shown in Figure 13, capital is abundant in the United States and relatively scarce in China and India. Returns on capital will be lower in the U.S. than in China and India; the relative price of capital goods will be higher in China and India than the United States.

Creating a single open market by opening trade will create incentives for capital owners to redeploy capital out of the U.S. and into China and India. This will take place through foreign direct investment (FDI) and portfolio investment. Capital redeployment redresses the imbalance over time, reducing the return differential and forcing returns to converge over time.[7]

## Figure 14: Arbitrage—Human Capital

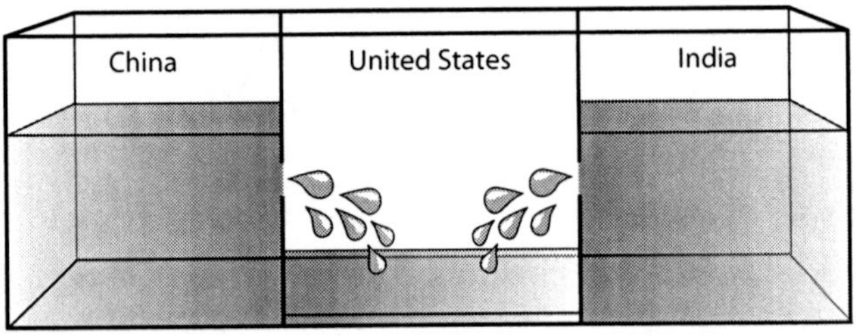

The situation seen from the point of view of an owner of human capital is depicted in Figure 14. Human capital is abundant in China and India relative to the U.S.; wages and incomes are lower in Asia than in the United States. Linking the three nations through trade will result in a net flow of human capital from Asia to the U.S., raising wages in China and India relative to the price of capital goods while lowering relative wages in the United States. The influx of human capital into the U.S. will take the form of immigration (legal or illegal), outsourcing work and imports of goods and services, which embody stored human work.

Economists typically describe trade-driven resource adjustments as smooth and gradual. That may have made sense when resource rede-

---

[7] American investors may not see this. The financial statements of U.S. public companies report the profits and returns of companies listed in America, not the returns on capital deployed in America. Capital redeployment is one of the major reasons why U.S. companies have been reporting record profits as a percentage of GDP in recent years.

ployments principally took place as international trade in physical goods. After all, potential resource transfers can be very large relative to the capacity of the communication channel linking the systems. For example, it takes two weeks to load goods onto a ship in Shanghai, sail it to Los Angeles and unload the cargo; and the number of containers a ship can carry is limited by its designed capacity, currently less than 14,000 standard 20-foot containers for the largest ships. Traditional trade adjustments drive prices together only gradually over many years.

Modern communications networks have changed all this. Optical fiber networks now connect the service sectors, or information economies, of rich and poor countries. This has dramatically accelerated trade and capital flows and increased the speed of economic change everywhere. In principle, trading services over optical fiber is like transporting goods on ships of infinite capacity that travel at the speed of light. The resulting quickening of economic change has important implications for economic and political stability.

## Non-Equilibrium Thermodynamics (NET)

Through most of its history, thermodynamics has assumed that adjustments toward thermal equilibrium were smooth and gradual; such adjustments are known as "reversible thermodynamic change." Reversible change assumes that the distance from equilibrium is very small—the gradient is almost flat—and that adjustment takes place at infinitesimally slow speed, just like the container ships in the previous section.

According to 1977 Nobelist Ilya Prigogine (1997), attempts by researchers to examine the behavior of systems far from equilibrium— including those of his Professor at the Free University of Brussels, the brilliant Belgian chemist Theophile de Donder—were actively discouraged within the physics and chemistry professions during the early decades of the 20th century. This is unfortunate, because far from equilibrium is where all the interesting behavior of thermodynamic systems takes place, as Prigogine later proved in his work on dissipative systems.

*Ilya Prigogine*[8]

Path-breaking recent work by Prigogine and his colleagues, known as "the Brussels School," showed that we are living in a world of irreversible non-equilibrium processes, and that distance from equilibrium is a fundamental parameter of nature. As the distance from equilibrium—and the corresponding temperature, pressure, or energy gradient—increases beyond a certain point, known as the bifurcation point, qualitative changes in system behavior appear that lead to abrupt, unpredictable and discontinuous change. They produce completely new coherent structures, which Prigogine referred to as "dissipative systems." When the distance from equilibrium increases still further beyond a second critical point, randomness forcefully reappears in a regime characterized by erratic behavior; this is the chaotic, unpredictable behavior that engineers refer to as turbulence.

Today, this dynamic new field of study is variously called chaos theory, complexity, complex adaptive systems, network theory, self-organizing systems, emergence, non-equilibrium thermodynamics, or simply NET. It is especially valuable for thinking through questions of stability, turbulence and system failure.

---

[8] Photo courtesy of Maryna Prigogine and the Center for Complex Quantum Systems (formerly the Ilya Prigogine Center for Studies in Statistical Mechanics and Complex Systems), University of Texas at Austin.

For more detail, see the work of Barabasi (2002), Buchanan (2002), Gleick (1987), Holland (1995), Kauffman (1993), Nicolis and Prigogine (1989), Prigogine (1997), Schneider and Sagan (2005), Strogatz (2003), Watts (2002), Watts (2003a), and Watts (2003b).

The father of them all, however, is Irwin Schrödinger's (1944) little book, *What is Life?*, based on three lectures he delivered at Trinity College, Dublin in 1943. This book arguably spawned both molecular biology and NET, the science of creating order from disorder.

Today's networked global economy is certainly far from equilibrium, as measured by price, wage, or return differentials, making non-equilibrium thermodynamics extremely relevant for current policy analysis. Nations today are not only connected by slow-moving ships of limited capacity; they are connected by fiber-optic communications networks, which can transport vast amounts of resources at the speed of light. These links have dramatically increased the responsiveness of the global economy to price and return differentials. The resulting capital flows, outsourcing, cross-border M&A, supply-chain and restructuring activities have also generated political backlash in many countries—the social manifestation of turbulence—raising important questions of economic and political stability.

In my book, *A Monetarist Model of Inflationary Expectations* (1973), I outlined a formal model of the information market. My conclusion was that economies of scale in information processing would eventually drive transaction costs to zero, making rapid price change inevitable. Transactions costs have since fallen by more than 90 percent—in Boltzmann's language, they can no longer be counted on to serve as an effective buffer on the speed of price changes. This has some very obvious and significant implications. Price disequilibria—markets, in other words—will be more erratic and volatile. Historical volatility estimates will consistently underestimate future volatility. And options pricing models, which rely on historical volatility measures, will consistently underprice risk.

NET has particularly interesting things to say about recessions, asset price bubbles and other temporary market failures. All are system or network properties that, in general, cannot be understood by reductionist analysis of the behavior of sub-groups of market participants. In other words, Y = C+I+G may be true as an accounting identity,[9] but it is likely to be useless for forecasting recessions that can be better understood as temporary network "blackouts." Recessions, as we will discuss in Chapter 7, occur when the information network we call a market economy temporarily stops processing information—usually the result of an intervention by a policy maker such as credit rationing, fuel rationing, or the imposition of quotas, which result in a situation of temporary non-price rationing.

NET also has important things to say about innovation and entrepreneurial behavior. Although economists write about the "animal spirits" of the entrepreneur, I suspect that entrepreneurship is a system property rather than an example of Darwinian natural selection. A recently discovered paper by Joseph Schumpeter (2005), written in 1932 but first published in the *American Economic Review* in March 2005, shows that he ultimately came to a similar view.

## Turbulence

Leonhard Euler, the Swiss mathematician and physicist, revolutionized the analysis of fluid dynamics in 1753 when he derived the set of partial differential equations that describe the motion of a fluid of zero viscosity (Johnson, 1998). Figure 15(a) illustrates the flow of such a non-viscous fluid around a cylinder (Acheson, 1990). Actual fluids be-

---

[9] Y=C+I+G is an accounting identity used in macroeconomics to describe a closed economy, where Y=GDP, C=Consumption, I=Investment and G=Government Spending. For an open economy, the identity becomes Y=C+I+G+(X-IM) where X=Exports, IM=Imports and the quantity (X-IM) represents net exports.

have very differently due to friction, as shown by the diagram of a real fluid with positive but small viscosity flowing past a cylinder in Figure 15(b) (van Dyke, 1982). The area downstream (to the right of) the cylinder is characterized by chaotic turbulence. Viscous flows are not, in general, reversible.

### Figure 15: Fluid Motion Past a Cylinder

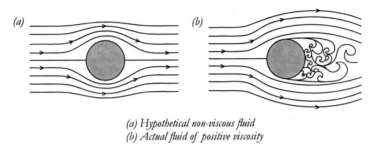

*(a) Hypothetical non-viscous fluid*
*(b) Actual fluid of positive viscosity*

Increasing velocity beyond a certain point leads to turbulence. Figure 16 shows drawings from experiments conducted by Osborne Reynolds in 1883. Reynolds marked the water drawn through a tube with a streak of visible dye to study the fluid motion. At very low velocity, the flow was smooth, or laminar, as shown in the top tube.

### Figure 16: Reynolds Experiments in Fluid Motion

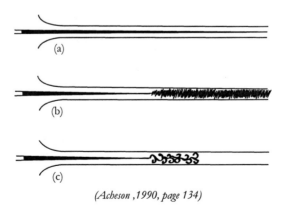

*(Acheson, 1990, page 134)*

As the velocity increased, however, there was always a point at which an arbitrarily small further increase in velocity would cause the flow to transition from laminar flow to turbulence, as shown in the middle tube—which was revealed to be a mass of more or less distinct curls when lit by an electric spark, as shown in Figure 16(c). According to Acheson (1990, page 134), "this sudden transition from laminar flow to turbulence as the speed is gradually increased is still one of the deepest problems in classical physics."

This transition from laminar flow to turbulence is well-known by engineers. Figure 17 shows that excessive velocity, sharp changes of direction and obstacles that impede flow can create turbulence, which erodes the tube and fitting, damaging the system. Less obviously, turbulence reduces flow pressure by narrowing the effective diameter of the tube used to transport fluid; pressure loss varies approximately with the square of flow velocity.

### Figure 17: Laminar Flow (a) and Turbulence (b)

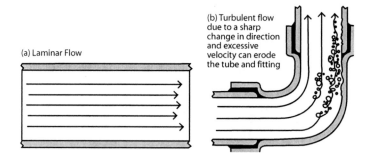

(a) Laminar Flow

(b) Turbulent flow due to a sharp change in direction and excessive velocity can erode the tube and fitting

*(Canadian Copper & Brass Association)*

Just as increasing velocity and sharp changes in direction can produce turbulence in the flow of physical fluids, increases in the velocity of trade and capital flows, as well as sharp changes in direction of employment patterns and incomes, can create turbulence in human societies in the form of political unrest and social instability. Social turbulence leads to pressures for protectionist policies that promise to return the society to its former stable condition. As we will see below, these are false promises.

## Accelerating Growth—Rising Protectionism

The high-speed communication networks and reduced costs of redeploying capital discussed earlier in this chapter have increased international trade and capital flows, as shown in Figure 18. They have also increased growth. Global economic growth was an incredible 5.4% in 2006, compared with 2.9% during 1950-1973 when Europe and Japan were rebuilding their economies after the war, and quadruple the 1.3% global growth during the 1870-1913 industrial revolution.

Figure 18: Rising Trade and Capital Flows

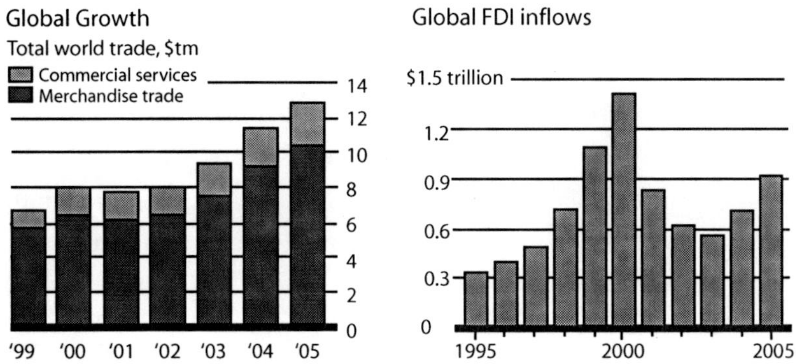
Global Growth
Total world trade, $tm
Commercial services
Merchandise trade
14
12
10
8
6
4
2
0
'99
'00
'01
'02
'03
'04
'05
Global FDI inflows
$1.5 trillion
1.2
0.9
0.6
0.3
0
1995
2000
2005

*(WTO, UNCTAD)*

Strong growth and capital redeployment towards fast-growing emerging markets like China and India have sharply increased profits as a share of GDP, as shown in Figure 19, and supported sustained increases in stock prices and net worth, especially in emerging market countries.

## Figure 19: Rising Global Profit
*G7 Corporate Profits as % of GDP*

*(UBS)*

As the previous section suggests, however, rapid growth and accelerating trade and investment flows produce turbulence in social systems as well, in the form of economic and social instability. This is the source of rising protectionist pressures around the world today.

There is always a certain level of protectionist background noise in international trade and finance, as politically powerful industries use government influence to jockey for advantage over foreign rivals. In recent years, however, the noise level has become deafening as country after country has moved to adopt rules limiting free trade and investment flows. Selected examples include:

1. In 2002, ahead of the mid-term elections, the U.S. imposed a 30% tariff on Canadian lumber and imported steel. Congress passed legislation making it illegal to sell catfish imported from Vietnam using the name "catfish," provoking retaliation from the EU and Japan.

2. In 2005, the U.S. Congress effectively blocked the announced acquisition of Unocal by CNOOC, the Chinese oil company, citing national security concerns even though Unocal's gas reserves were located in Indonesia. In early 2006, a second uproar in Congress blocked UAE company Dubai Ports World from acquiring the U.S. port management interests of British company P&O.

3. In 2007, Carlyle, the U.S. private investment firm, was forced to scale back its announced acquisition of China's Xugong Construction Machinery to a minority stake following intense political pressure. Chinese leaders cited national security worries.

4. U.S. protectionist moves against China are accelerating fast. China announced the end of the fixed RMB/$ policy in July 2005 in order to a) accommodate growing pressure from the U.S. regarding the U.S. trade deficit with China, and b) to deflect pressure in the U.S. Congress to pass China-targeted protectionist legislation, endorsed by Senators Schumer and Graham. More recently, the U.S. blocked Chinese fish imports and U.S. media focused on quality problems in Chinese goods.

5. China retaliated by blocking shipments of mineral water, orange pulp and pistachios, citing quality and health issues.

6. Germany has drawn up plans to stop strategic assets—including telecom, banks, post, energy and logistics—from being sold to foreign sovereign investment funds and "finance houses," i.e., private equity and hedge funds.

7. French President Sarkozy succeeded in striking the words "free and undistorted competition" from the EU's treaty objectives in 2007.

8. Italy blocked the acquisition of Telecom Italia by Spain's Telefonica SA, forcing the buyer to team up with three local partners.

9. Canada is considering restricting foreign acquisitions after last year's purchase of steelmaker Dofasco by France's Arcelor.

10. Russia is preparing a list of 39 strategic sectors, including natural resources and technology, where foreign ownership will be limited.

11. Venezuela is nationalizing its telecom sector; Bolivia is nationalizing its energy sector.

## Figure 20: Impact of Protectionism on Foreign Direct Investment
*Percentage of changes to investment regulations that were less favorable to FDI*

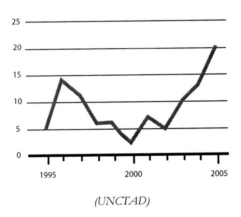

*(UNCTAD)*

There are still free trade voices, of course, including EU Internal Market Commissioner McCreevy and new British Prime Minister Gordon Brown. Unfortunately, their voices are increasingly drowned out by protectionists. So far, the damage is hard to see. Economic growth is still strong and FDI flows are robust. M&A transactions involving two countries separated by differing language, law, culture, currency and steering-wheel placement are at all-time highs. In the first half of 2007, the number of cross border transactions increased 17% compared with the same period in 2006. But investment regulations are beginning to move against global investors, as Figure 20 shows.

I am convinced that today's chorus of protectionist actions represents more than the profit-seeking actions of a few special interest groups. Today, when a political leader announces a new protectionist measure, crowds cheer. I believe that rising protectionism, nationalism and social instability are rooted in the turbulence caused by rapid economic change. Rapid economic change raises average incomes, creates new industries and destroys others, and changes the lives of many people. Those whose fortunes have been temporarily or permanently reduced, as well as those who are simply afraid of change, will appeal to the political process for relief; political leaders who promise to stop or reverse change will gain power over leaders who counsel openness. These barriers slow economic activity by making arbitrage less profitable—roughly the same as an increase in Boltzmann's activation energy threshold.

Left unchecked, this process can lead to global trade war as country after country erects non-market barriers to the smooth flow of trade. Ultimately, these mounting frictions can produce system failure, akin to the blackouts caused by failure of an electricity network. As Hayek and von Mises first pointed out, markets are exquisitely efficient information networks that solve a society's division of knowledge problem by selectively transmitting information on relative wants and scarcities to only those people who need the information—using symbols we call prices.[10] When non-market intervention prevents prices from carrying information, (for example, non-price rationing caused by price controls), the system breaks down.

---

[10] We will discuss the work of Hayek and von Mises in greater depth in Chapter 7: Network Failures and the Information Economy.

Rampant protectionism could also breed social and political instability and ultimately bring nations into conflict. Political instability would put all the gains in reducing poverty over the past quarter century at risk. Schneider & Sagan (2005) argue that complex non-equilibrium thermodynamic systems—societies, political systems, ecosystems and economies—share a universal feature: they regress to earlier, more hierarchical, less complex and less open forms of organization under conditions of environmental stress (plagues, wars and depressions) when turbulence reduces energy flow.

This system property is known as the Savonarola Effect (Bloom, 1997), after the 15th century Dominican priest whose fiery sermons against the corrupt Catholic Church incited Florence mobs to burn books and works of art. Savonarola was, in turn, burned at the stake by the church in 1498. History contains countless examples of the Savonarola Effect. We see it today as the Patriot Act, wiretapping and immigration restrictions following the September 11, 2001 terrorist attacks in the United States.

While the unintended consequences of protectionism would be harmful for people living in developed countries, they would be a tragedy for the world's three billion people who still worry about having enough food every day.

We can choose a better course. As our framework shows, turbulence is a natural and unavoidable by-product of rapid global growth. Although we cannot eliminate protectionism, there are things we can do to retard its growth and mitigate its harmful effects. I have outlined some policies to help accomplish these goals below.

## Policy Recommendations

The laws of thermodynamics are the one set of laws that all humans must obey—with no exceptions. This leads to some general conclusions:

1. Just as there is the second law of thermodynamics, there is a law of thermo-economics that drives all economic change. Price and return differentials—price gradients—cause resources to flow from places where they are relatively abundant to places where they are relatively scarce.

2. Likewise, economics is affected by the laws of acceleration. High-speed communications networks and efficient global capital markets increase the velocity of resource flows. This has created today's unprecedented growth of global GDP, profits and wealth.

3. Economics is also subject to the laws of turbulence. Turbulence is an unavoidable and natural by-product of rapid growth.

4. Faster change has created turbulence in both developed and emerging economies due to frictions that make it difficult to change behavior quickly. Turbulence has given rise to today's climate of growing protectionism. It cannot be wished away, but it can be mitigated.

5. Reducing frictions does not eradicate turbulence. It does, however, allow a system to grow smoothly at a higher rate before experiencing turbulence, making turbulence less costly.

6. Policies to reduce frictions include training, education, portable pension and health care benefits, and relocation as-

sistance for people experiencing change due to rapid global growth.

7. An education system that gives people the tools to adapt to change by emphasizing transferable skills and problem solving, as opposed to rote learning, will reduce turbulence.

8. Labor market policies that make it easy for companies and workers to change the nature of the work they do in response to changing market forces will reduce turbulence.

9. Policies that increase people's overall sense of security, such as reducing corruption, predictable rule of law and a healthy environment with clean air and water, will reduce friction and turbulence.

10. A stable monetary environment—including a stable price level, a stable exchange rate and a stable tax system—will reduce turbulence.

11. Policy makers who want to reduce turbulence must anticipate retaliation from other nations. To do so, they must thoroughly understand other nations' political and economic systems.

The framework in this chapter is based on science. Ultimately, however, science is about people. The reason we care about protectionism is its impact on the lives of families trying to feed, educate and care for their children to give them a better future. Protectionism attempts to stop change—but change is inevitable. Our resources woujld be better used to prepare people for change by giving them a stable society, a growing economy and forward-looking education that teaches them the skills and flexibility that they will need for the jobs of tomorrow's global economy.

## Energy Shortage or Knowledge Shortage?

Strong growth and rising energy needs are increasing the world's reliance on oil and gas energy supplies from the troubled Middle East, making energy security an urgent issue for many countries. Existing policies, based on orthodox demand-based economics and an overly narrow concept of energy, are unlikely to solve the problem. This section uses the framework presented earlier in this chapter to look at unconventional solutions to the energy security problem, including communication networks, information technology, education, agricultural research and legal, regulatory, and exchange rate policies.

Rising economic activity has increased global oil and gas demand faster than the growth of supplies. This is increasing our reliance on coal supplies, which has costly implications for air and water resources. And it is increasing the world's reliance on oil and gas imports from the troubled and potentially unstable Middle East, where the lion's share of the world's known oil and gas reserves are located.

### Figure 21: Proved Oil Reserves at end 2005
*(thousand million barrels)*

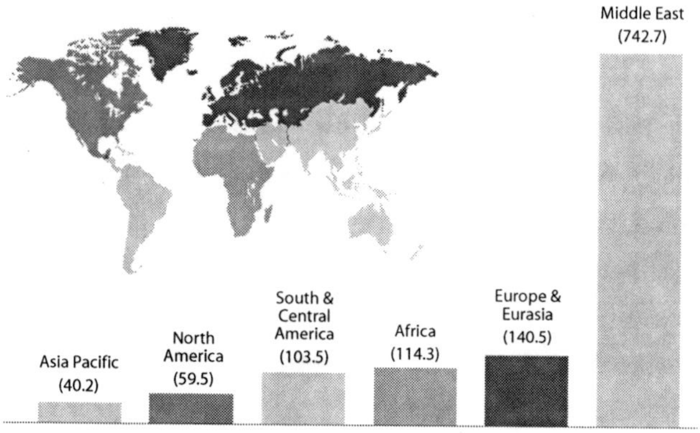

*(Davies, 2006, page 3)*

## Figure 22: Proved Natural Gas Reserves at end 2005
*(trillions of cubic meters)*

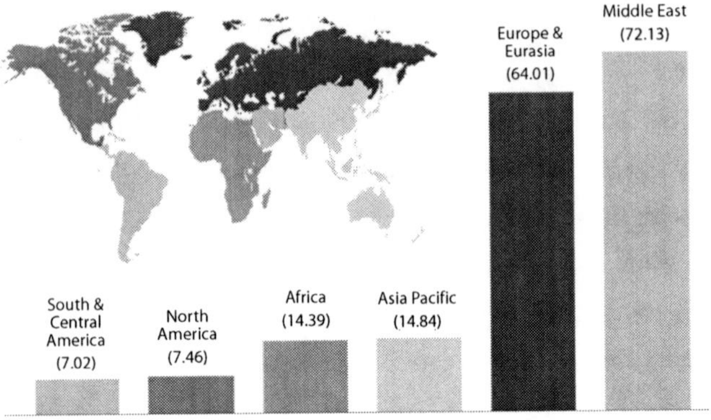

*(Davies, 2006, page 18)*

Without secure future energy supplies, a nation cannot provide its people with the stable political and economic environment that underpins strong and sustainable economic growth. This is especially important for Asian nations, where the imbalance between scarce energy resources, large populations and growing incomes is greater than in other areas.

For both high-income nations and emerging economies, whose people have now tasted rising incomes, halting growth is not an option. Energy security—securing long-term access to the energy resources that can provide sustainable long-term growth and rising living standards—has become an urgent matter for governments everywhere.

Some governments are taking steps to attack the energy security problem by increasing exploration for new resources, investing in resources outside their borders, undertaking long-term supply contracts, expanding use of nuclear power, investing in alternative fuel technologies and encouraging conservation.[11] Yet, in spite of great efforts and

---

[11] For a recent discussion of China's efforts to address energy security, see Amy Myers Jaffe and Matthew Chen, "Testimony Before the U.S. China Economic and Security Review Commission Hearing on China's Role in the World," August 4, 2006.

some successes, the Asian Development Bank's *Asian Development Outlook* forecasts rising Asian oil and gas imports in the years ahead.[12] The energy security problem grows larger every year. Access to energy resources is the most likely cause of future conflict among nations. Clearly, we need some new thinking to solve this problem.

The framework presented in the previous section provides a new way of thinking about the relationship between energy and growth, based on the broad concept of energy in the physical sciences and on the laws of thermodynamics. In this framework, resource flows between nations are driven by price and return gradients according to the second law of thermodynamics. Policies impact resource flows by impacting price and return gradients, providing incentives, or signals, for entrepreneurs to change their behavior.

This broader view of energy points toward unconventional structural solutions to the energy security problem, including: 1) investing in communication networks, information technology and education; 2) investing in agricultural research in order to utilize the solar energy captured by plants more efficiently, and so that we can improve the productivity of farm workers in order to release manpower to the energy-efficient and environmentally-friendly services sector; and 3) legal, regulatory and exchange rate policies to provide the stable economic and capital market environment needed to attract high-tech capital and technology.

## Energy Security

The thermodynamic framework presented in this chapter suggests fruitful areas for future discussion and research and has important applications regarding the question of energy security. In particular, it suggests that energy security should be analyzed with respect to the full

---

[12]   Asian Development Bank, *Asian Development Outlook 2007*, March, 2007.

economic, financial, political and social situation of a country, not just by counting up barrels of oil or cubic meters of gas.

I will define energy security as the situation where a national government has command over sufficient controllable stores of energy to maintain, with a high level of confidence, stable and rising living standards for its people over time—the prerequisites for maintaining social and political order.

The critical words in this definition are "command" and "controllable." For example, a nation may have a long-term supply contract or even legal ownership rights over energy resources located in another nation, but may not *control* them because supply contracts and legal rights may not be enforceable without resorting to military conflict in times of crisis when they are most needed. In this case, a seller continues to hold an implicit real option to "call" for delivery of the resources in specific situations. Energy reserves are bulky and difficult to transport and store. Aside from modest strategic reserves, you can buy them, but you can't bring them home.

Resources located within a country's national borders are likely to be more controllable, but even then they may be subject to intervention from foreign governments—witness Japanese activities in Manchuria in the 1930s and recent activities in the Gulf Region. Secure energy resources must be both controllable and defendable.

A nation's most controllable resources are its endowments of natural resources, the physical capital within its borders and the energies and knowledge of its people.

Governments today are pursuing various strategies to move toward energy security, including building strategic petroleum reserves, acquiring reserves in foreign countries, undertaking long-term supply contracts, exploring for additional reserves both inside their borders and offshore, forging alliances with countries rich in oil and gas, investing in pipelines, LNG ports and other distribution infrastructure, and implementing policies designed to encourage investment in solar, wind, water, and biofuels, to make more effective use of coal deposits, and to encourage conservation. I would suggest that, with few exceptions, such policies have too narrow a focus on fossil fuels—and place excessive reliance on collecting current solar flux, as opposed to mining alternative sources of stored energy.

The thermodynamic framework suggests a broader definition of energy and indicates that we should use our human energies to find ways to improve the efficiency with which we capture, mine, store, attract and deploy solar energy to produce economic activity. Fortunately, as outlined in previous sections, there are ample opportunities to improve efficiencies in all these areas.

## Strategies to Increase Flux

Economists will be tempted to try to solve the energy security problem, of course, by simply assuming increased solar radiation. Conjectures about positioning mirrors at stable points in outer space, explored by some scientists, seem impractical. But it is not impractical to acknowledge evidence, reported by Singer (2007), showing that solar radiation has indeed increased by .05% per decade since the 1970s, an amount roughly equal to total human energy consumption. This increase in solar flux will increase crop yields through increased photosynthesis.

## Strategies to Increase Our Ability to Capture Solar Energy

This is an area of research with great promise. Research areas include:

1. Large-scale collection of solar energy in desert regions, which can be used to produce hydrogen

2. Developing new varieties of chlorophyll to increase the ability of plant matter to harvest more energy from the sun (Atkins, 1994)

3. Genetic engineering of crops to suppress the photorespiration that wastes as much as half of the carbon captured by photosynthesis, which would increase crop yields by allowing plants to process carbon dioxide more efficiently (Atkins, 1994)

4. Research on the beneficial effects of higher recent temperatures and increased carbon dioxide levels on crop yields (Singer, 2007)

5. Research on environmentally safe fertilizers, insecticides, and fungicides to increase crop yields and reduce manpower needed for growing food

6. Genetically-engineered seeds that improve crop yield, resist drought, insects and disease, and have increased levels of protein and amino acids that are critical for human nutrition, like the Quality-Protein (QP) maize developed at Mexico's International Maize and Wheat Improvement Center (Singer, 2007)

7. Biotech-modified corn, cotton and soybean crops, like the new pest-resistant hybrid cotton that has been genetically engineered in China and which has freed up 600,000 hectares (almost 1.5 million acres) of land for growing food (Singer, 2007)

8. Infrastructure projects to improve irrigation and control flood damage, improving crop yields

These research topics increase our ability to store solar energy in the form of plant life. All increase the productivity of agricultural labor, freeing up manpower to grow the energy-friendly service sector.

## Strategies to Increase Our Ability to Mine Stored Solar Energy

The oil, gas and coal reserves reported in official statistics only reflect the amounts that can be economically extracted at current market prices. This leaves out vast amounts of resources in economically depleted fields and low-yield tar sand deposits. Asian nations have a wonderful opportunity to use their most abundant resource—human capital—to develop technologies for improving recovery yields from existing oil fields. This can be done in partnership with the governments of the Gulf Region and in countries that are rich in fossil fuels, but do not have sufficient populations to conduct the research, by setting up joint research laboratories at leading Chinese and Indian Universities. The same human capital resources can be used to solve Feynman's call for a sustainable alternative energy solution from earlier in this chapter, by investing in research on economically producing hydrogen, controllable nuclear fusion and other forms of usable energy.

## Strategies to Attract Stored Energy

Another strategy for increasing energy security is to become a destination resort for stored energy in all its forms. Like a photon, a capital good is a quantum unit of stored energy. The same is true for a scientist, an R&D lab, or a scientific discovery. Government policies can alter the likelihood that existing stored energy located around the world will migrate to their countries. Like the bacteria that once lived as parasites within our cells but decided to take up permanent residence as mitochondria, foreign capital, foreign-developed technology and foreign-born human capital improve energy security. Policies to attract foreign sources of stored energy include:

1.  Political and social stability

2. Rule of law, methods for enforcing contracts and settling disputes, property rights and intellectual property protection

3. Legal and accounting environment, lack of corruption and trust in public institutions and public officials

4. Tax laws, infrastructure and education

5. Visas and immigration restrictions

6. Communications networks

7. Stable currency, inflation and growth

8. Capital markets

9. Media access and free flow of information

In each case, when deciding whether to welcome foreign stores of energy into our country, there is a simple test—do they bring more energy into the country than they will consume? Or in other words, will doing so result in a net increase in our supply of stored energy and our ability to do work?

## Strategies to Increase Our Ability to Convert Energy into Economic Activity

The final strategies I will mention are perhaps both the easiest to achieve and have the most impact—policies that make a nation more efficient at converting energy into economic activity. These strategies increase worker productivity and increase incomes for a given supply of energy. In doing so, they make a nation more energy independent.

Primary industries, such as mining and agriculture, use a great deal of fossil fuel per unit of output. Secondary industries, such as manufacturing, use less energy. Tertiary, or service, industries use the least energy of all. For this reason, strategies that improve productivity in agriculture, mining and manufacturing, thereby leading to the redeployment of manpower to the service industries, reduce the amount of fossil fuel needed to produce each unit of output—making a nation more energy independent.

These policies are based on the notion that human capital, physical capital and technology can, and should, be viewed as sources of energy, no different in principal than oil, gas and coal reserves.

## Conclusion

The 20th century was the century of dinosaur energy; the 21st century will be dominated by human capital. Investing in human capital is the only path to rising incomes, energy security and truly sustainable growth. To tap that resource, governments need to invest in educating their people to the highest level—especially in math, science, and foreign languages—and in building the fiber-optic communications networks that will allow the work produced by their human capital to be distributed quickly and inexpensively to end-users around the world. To remain competitive, a country must be at the forefront of research and development in new energy and information technologies. In the end, the productivity of a country's people is the only true path to energy security.

# 7

# Network Failures and the
# Information Economy

One of the rules of science is that if you think up anything good, somebody else has already invented it. That's especially true when you work on topics that Friedrich von Hayek wrote about—which means all of them. This chapter's topic is neural networks.[1]

I once heard a famous neuroscientist say that if the brain were simple enough to understand, we would be too dumb to understand it. I can't remember his name. I guess that makes his point.

Our brain's capacity is also extremely limited relative to the job we ask it to do every day. Our brain not only has to run our sensory system so that we can see, hear, smell, taste and touch; it also has to run our motor system so that we can walk, talk and chew gum. And then there are all

---

[1] There is a fascinating new field called computational neurology that focuses on such issues. The best place to start to learn about it is to read Montague's (2006) book, *Why Choose This Book?*, which contains a thorough review of the neuroscience literature. Also see Churchland and Sejnowski's (1992) *The Computational Brain* for a technical treatment.

the other comforts we have grown used to, such as breathing, heartbeat, body temperature and reproduction. And, of course, we have to make decisions—about which socks to put on in the morning, what to have for dinner at night and which stocks to put in our portfolios.

Brains deal with this overwhelming workload by creating patterns, or metaphors, to reduce complicated information sets down to simple ones for storage and by using rules of thumb—Kahneman and Tversky (1982) refer to them as heuristics—to make decisions. This relatively new field of research, known as *behavioral economics*,[2] as well as its first cousin, *behavioral finance*,[3] examines how real people behave, rather than the representative automatons with perfect knowledge that we call the "economic man." Both fields can be viewed as offshoots of evolutionary science, a broad field ranging from evolutionary biology[4] to *evolutionary economics*.[5]

Rules of thumb do a pretty good job during normal times, i.e., times when things turn out just like they were when we loaded the rules of thumb into our mental libraries, known as *metaphor banks*. But they are responsible for important, systematic errors during unusual times, which unfortunately is just when we most need them.

This is especially important for economics because, as Hayek wrote 70 years ago, a market economy is nothing more than a vast, parallel-processing information network that processes far too much information for any one person to understand.

---

[2]   The classic reference is Kahneman, Slovik and Tversky's *Judgment Under Uncertainty: Heuristics and Biases* (1982).

[3]   Richard Peterson (2007) reviews the main findings of behavioral finance in *Inside the Investor's Brain*.

[4]   See E.O. Wilson's *Sociobiology* (1975).

[5]   Dopfer's (2005) text *The Evolutionary Foundation of Economics* contains a wonderful collection of articles. Beinhocker (2006), *The Origin of Wealth: Evolution, Complexity, and the Radical Remaking of Economics*, does a good job weaving the evolutionary economics literature together with the literature on complex systems. Lotka's (1924) *Elements of Mathematical Biology* and (1934) *Analytical Theory and Biological Populations* were the first major attempts to apply systems mathematics to biology and to the analysis of *epigenesis*, the co-development of biological populations. Odum (1971) applied systems principles to study the way a system of co-dependent populations processes energy.

Recent developments in network and information theory can help us understand the mortgage crisis and the credit problems we are living through today. Network theory studies the behavior of interconnected systems,[6] such as a power grid, the internet, a community of insects[7] or an economy.

Network theory helps us understand *cascading network failures*, a situation in which the failure of a single node leads to the shutdown of an entire network. The best example of a cascading network failure that we have all experienced is a power blackout during a storm. The wind knocks down a single power line, which leads to the loss of power for an entire city.

Bill Miller, Legg Mason's legendary mutual fund manager and vice chairman of the Santa Fe Institute, once advised me to read a book on network theory written by Albert Barabasi (2002) called *Linked*. When a brilliant person advises me to read something, my practice is to walk directly to the nearest Barnes & Noble and get started. I was not disappointed. Barabasi reviews the development of network theory from its beginning with Leonard Euler in 1736. He then uses network theory to explain the great Northeast blackout of 1965, the 1996 blackout of 11 Western U.S. states and two Canadian provinces, and the East Asian crisis of 1997. If he were writing the book today, Barabasi would certainly

---

[6] I have always been interested in the behavior of interconnected systems. On the *Rutledge Capital* website's "JR's Bookshelf" page, you will find references to a number of books about plagues, which is perhaps the most compelling application of network, or system theory. One of the important questions about networks, especially in epidemiology, is *percolation theory*, which asks how fast, and under what conditions, a signal (disease) percolates across a network. During the plague in Europe at the end of the fifteenth century, which killed a quarter of the population, the answer was seven miles per day—about the distance a sick person can walk in a day.

[7] The classic work is Holldobler and Wilson's (1990) fascinating study, *The Ants*. In Deborah Gordon's (2000) *Ants at Work: How an Insect Society is Organized*, Gordon showed that ant colonies behave as complex systems. Perhaps her most compelling observation is that old ant colonies are much less likely to engage in conflict with neighboring colonies, even though no worker is more than one year old and there is no communication between the queen and the workers.

include the bursting of the dot-com bubble and the subprime mortgage meltdown that is still with us today.

Barabasi writes that cascading network failures such as these are properties of the system architecture of highly connected networks. It is pointless to search for the "cause" of a specific instance of system failure. In complex networks, the breakdown of some well-selected nodes sets off a cascade of failures that can shake the whole system—this is the Achilles' heel of all complex networks. Unfortunately, we do not know how to prevent them. Barabasi explains: "Despite these advances, our understanding of cascading failures is rather limited. Topological robustness is a structural feature of networks. Cascading failures, however, are a dynamic property of complex systems, a relatively uncharted territory" (page 121).

Today, we are living through a cascading network failure—a blackout—in the capital markets. I don't need to write "temporary" blackout because everyone knows that *all* blackouts are temporary. Blackouts always catch us by surprise—they are unpredictable by definition. And *black-ins* always catch us by surprise too, when the lights come back on just after we have located the flashlight, the candles and the matches.

To understand the economy as an information network, we have to go back 70 years to Hayek's two classic papers on knowledge: *Economics and Knowledge* (his 1936 Presidential address to the London Economics Club) and *The Use of Knowledge in Society* (1945). Hayek's papers are both reprinted in *Individualism and Economic Order* (1948). These two papers will do more to help you understand today's subprime mortgage crisis than reading any other written analysis I know, including this one.[8]

---

[8]   Hayek actually invented the concept of a neural network—he called it a neural system—in a paper he wrote as a young student in 1919, and later published as *The Sensory Order* (1952). Hayek's book is brilliant, but utterly opaque, at least to me. Perhaps that explains why D. O. Hebb's (1949) book, *The Organization of Behavior*, is the standard citation. Hebb, himself, defined a classic as "a work that is often cited but never read."

In *Economics and Knowledge*, Hayek exposes the fact that the concept of equilibrium in economics is a tautology. "It seems that the skeleton in our cupboard, the 'economic man,' whom we have exorcised with prayer and fasting, has returned through the back door in the form of a quasi-omniscient individual. The statement that, if people know everything, they are in equilibrium is true simply because that is how we define equilibrium" (page 46). The most interesting question, wrote Hayek, is who needed to possess what information; a question von Mises referred to as the problem of the *division of knowledge*. The central question of economics, according to Hayek, is the following: "How can the combination of fragments of knowledge existing in different minds bring about results which, if they were to be brought about deliberately, would require a knowledge on the part of the directing mind which no single person can possess?" (page 54).

Later, in *The Use of Knowledge in Society*, Hayek argues that man has solved this problem by designing the price system, a mechanism for transmitting information that uses a symbol, which we call price, to transmit *only the most essential information about changes in wants and scarcities to only those people who need it.* "It is more than a metaphor to describe the price system as a kind of machinery for registering change, or a system of telecommunications" (page 87). Without this price system to economize information requirements, a society based on division of labor could not be sustained.

Market economies rely on prices to transmit information across the information network we call the economy. When something happens to interfere with this flow of information, markets experience blackouts—just like the cascading network failures discussed by Barabasi. We call them bubbles, meltdowns, crises, recessions or depressions. They are an essential feature of market economies. We are experiencing one today.

## The Subprime Mortgage Crisis

I have lived through a number of market blackouts during my career. Today's subprime mortgage crisis is just the most recent one. It is neither the most interesting blackout I have seen nor is it unique.

Most market commentators today are talking about recession. They worry that falling home prices will cause consumers to reduce spending, which will lead to a recession. This is the wrong thing to worry about. The subprime mortgage crisis is a capital market story, not a recession story. That's where its solution will lie.

Forget the GDP accounts that you learned about in macroeconomics class. As we discussed in Chapter 3, the big economic and financial earthquakes always take place in the asset markets. Policy actions that target spending, like the checks mailed out this spring by President Bush and Congressional leaders, are not going to solve the problem.

When most people talk about the economy, they mean gross domestic product (GDP), which measures the market value of the goods and services produced during a given year or quarter. This is a rough estimate of the value of the work produced by the economy over that period, as I outlined in Chapter 6.

GDP seems like a pretty big number to most people. In 2007, U.S. nominal GDP, using current market prices, was $13.8 trillion at an annual rate. Changes in GDP, which we use to measure growth, are much smaller. In the first quarter of 2008, real GDP increased by an annual rate of $111 billion from the previous quarter.

It is important to remember that the numbers in the GDP accounts are all measured at annual rates, which means that they tell us what GDP would be over a full year if all four quarters of the year looked exactly like this one. That means that nominal GDP actually only increased by about $28 billion (one quarter of the $111 billion annual rate) during the quarter.

Compare these numbers with measures of privately-owned assets. According to the most recent *Flow of Funds Report* from the Federal Reserve Board, the market value of privately-owned U.S. assets at the end of Q3 2007 was roughly $195 trillion, or about 14 times the size of GDP. Because the numbers are so large, even a small disturbance in the asset markets—a change in people's relative demands to hold assets—can send shock waves through the economy that will dwarf anything going on in the GDP accounts.

What is happening in today's asset markets is not a GDP event; it is not the result of late mortgage payments. It is a blackout in the mortgage-backed securities market. Wealth-holders are simply unwilling to own the existing stock of assets. This blackout in the bond market is not going to be fixed by giving checks for $12, or $1200, to every man, woman and child in the country. The only way to fix the problem is to restore confidence in the underlying assets, which would restore the flow of information in the capital markets.

## The Stimulus Plan is a Dud

We might ask why Washington has suddenly erupted in a lovefest, with everyone in the government falling over themselves to send us money. Did somebody put something in the water? If they did, I certainly hope they publish the source on the official congressional website. I want to get some of that water.

All the leaders of both parties in Washington have one thing in common: they are all incumbents. They absolutely do not want voters to walk into the voting booths in November in the middle of a recession. It's bad for business.

Crafting the stimulus package is a great political opportunity for getting credit for $150 billion in "targeted," i.e. earmarked, handouts. Although my personal taste runs to tax cuts, this applies to both the spending and the tax cuts under discussion. Every politician is trying to carve off as much of the $150 billion for his or her people as possible. This is not a partisan statement; it applies to both Republicans and Democrats.

The package itself is a stew that consists of part checks to taxpayers, part checks to people who are currently not paying taxes at all, and part business cuts in the form of accelerated appreciation for capital purchases. Something for (almost) everyone.

And then there is the economics. The stimulus plans being talked about are old-fashioned, textbook, prime-the-pump fiscal amphetamines. Their objective is to get people to spend more money. They never work. The stimulus package won't do any material good for the economy—the numbers are just too small in a country where GDP is $14 trillion and Americans own $200 trillion worth of assets.

By trying to solve the wrong problem, our leaders are ignoring the right one. It's like being wheeled into the emergency room while you are having a heart attack and having the doctor come in wanting to discuss whether you should have a face lift or a tummy tuck.

The economy's real problem is not how to get consumers to spend more money—American consumers have proven they are good at spending money. It's how to get investors to own the stock of outstanding bonds and equities in the asset markets. The stock market and mortgage market problems are questions of visibility and valuation in the capital markets. Investors do not feel capable of estimating and valuing the cash flows from existing securities. They are not problems with consumer spending or mortgage payments. Capital market problems can only be fixed by giving investors visibility over those cash flows.

One way to do that would be to announce that White House and Congressional leaders have together decided to block all of the witch-hunt legislation that targets investors as scapegoats for the mortgage market collapse. That would include proposed revision of the bankruptcy laws to allow judges to rewrite mortgage contracts in any way they want,

as well as special measures encouraging people to sue the ultimate owners of mortgage securities—pension funds, insurance companies, banks
and individual investors. Witch hunts are making the problem worse.

The best way to encourage investors to own securities again, of
course, would be to give them visibility over tax rates, and therefore after-
tax income, over the life of the securities. That means making the 2003
capital gains and dividend tax cuts permanent so that investors can set
prices. This issue is worth more than 20%—or $3 trillion—to the value
of the stock market, and even more than that to the bond market. That
is what the markets were waiting to hear when the President announced
the stimulus package. The production economy—GDP—cannot stabilize until the capital markets begin to clear again.

I wrote the following piece about the specific details of the stimulus plan when it was announced in January.

—

President Bush announced today that the White House has reached
an agreement with Speaker Pelosi and Minority Leader Boehner on
the components of the economic growth package they have been
working on. The details of the package are outlined below:

1. Total package of just over $150 billion
2. $103 billion in checks will be mailed to 117 million families,
   including:
   a. Checks for $300 ($600 for those filing jointly) to people
      who earned at least $3,000
   b. An additional $300 check per child. (Go forth and mul-
      tiply)
   c. Checks for $600 ($1,200 for joint filers) for people who
      actually paid taxes last year

    d. Checks phased out for incomes above $75,000 ($150,000 for joint filers)

3.   $50 billion in business tax cuts including:

    a. One-year bonus appreciation

    b. Allowing small businesses to expense (instantly depreciate) up to $250,000 in capital spending this year. (The previous measure, which allowed expensing up to $125,000, expired in December)

    c. A temporary increase in the conforming loan limits for Fannie Mae and Freddie Mac from $417,000 to roughly $750,000, which would make mortgage loans in that size range easier to securitize and sell to investors

There were no tax increases in the package (duh!), no increase in unemployment benefits, no increase in food stamps and no additional public works spending projects.

Later in the day I was on a conference call with Ed Lazear, a very smart labor economist and Chairman of the President's Council of Economic Advisors, along with a number of other economists. Ed said they were comfortable it could be enacted quickly—Senators Reid and McConnell agreed before the deal was done that the House should take the lead on the package details. There will still be some brushfires—Senator Baucus has already indicated he wants more unemployment pay in the deal—but it will get done.

The Treasury believes that they can process the paperwork and get the first checks out in 60 days, which means most people will get checks in April or May.

Ed said they believe this will raise 2008 GDP by two-thirds to three-quarters of one percent. At today's $14 trillion GDP, that would be $94-105 billion.

I suggested that the problem with the economy is not getting people to spend money, but getting investors to own securities, which could be accomplished by giving investors better visibility over future cash flows. I asked whether there were any discussions about the damage being done by the Congressional witch hunt proposals targeted at investors. (No.) I asked why the most powerful medicine in the package—the increase in conforming loan limits—was made temporary, which would leave a year's worth of temporarily conforming loans stranded as orphans in the capital markets. (They thought the markets would price them efficiently.)

I don't agree. Making loans conformable means allowing them to be packaged and sold as commodities, which will improve their marketability to investors. But investors want to invest in a stream of loans, not one-time packages. And recent events show that there is a fatal flaw in the way the capital markets price securities. The dominant pricing methodology—variously known as Modern Portfolio Theory, CAPM, or Black-Scholes—assumes that markets are in equilibrium at all times. That is clearly not the case. It is the temporary breakdowns—the ones I have called blackouts—that are responsible for crises.

As I wrote recently, I don't believe the stimulus package will do a lot of good—at most, a half percent bump in GDP for one year and a roughly equivalent drop in the following year as businesses pay higher taxes again—but it won't do a great deal of harm either. We should keep our eyes on the process to make sure nobody slips anything else into the deck. I will be arguing very hard that, at the very least, they should make the increased loan limits permanent—it will cost nothing to do it and it would do a lot to unfreeze the mortgage market. Looks like the real stimulus package—making the 2003 tax rates permanent so people can value securities—is off the table for a while.

## The 2001 Credit Crunch and the Two-Cylinder Economy

The last time we had a good credit crunch was in 2001, when the bank regulators accidentally shut down the entire banking system—whoopsie—by forcing it into non-price rationing of business loans. I wrote the following song lyrics about what the crunch felt like to a business owner:

*Credit Crunch Blues*
*Woke up this mornin', feelin' for my shoes.*
*The bank man repossessed them. He took my old dog too.*
*I got the blues. I got the credit crunch blues.*
*Can't get me no collateral. I got the credit crunch blues.*
*(Guitar solo)*
*I busted all my covenants, defaulted on my debt.*
*The banker's in my face about as close as he can get.*
*I got the blues; I got the Credit Crunch blues.*
*Can't get me no recovery, I got the Credit Crunch blues.*

## How a Credit Crunch Works

I wrote an op-ed for the *Wall Street Journal* in November, 2001 arguing that reducing the federal funds rate would not save the economy from recession because bank regulators had frozen the business loan market like a fly in amber. The regulators took exception to my article and attacked me with a vengeance—I must have been onto something! The main points in my argument follow.

—

When the Federal Open Market Committee meets today, it won't be arguing over whether we are in recession. The economy is weaker today than at any time since 1982. It will almost certainly end the meeting by voting to reduce interest rates again. This will produce the same results as the previous rate cuts this year: absolutely none.

Interest rate cuts alone are not enough to jump-start this economy. We need to make sure that cheaper credit reaches the companies that need it. Credit rationing, not interest rates, is the real problem with the economy.

The Fed's monetary stimulus has been hijacked by the bank regulators. These credit highwaymen aren't bad guys; they are just doing their jobs. The Treasury Department's Office of the Comptroller of the Currency (OCC), which is charged with regulating federally chartered banks, has a different agenda from the Fed. Its job is to protect bank capital, not to protect the economy. It does so with an army of bank examiners, who wield the blunt instrument of credit rationing inside banks. For more than a year, these regulators have been diverting bank reserves into Treasury securities instead of business loans, in hopes of restoring bank capital that was damaged by technology lending. Companies that rely on banks for working capital have been sucking air.

To restore growth, we need a functioning banking system. This will require a level of coordination the Treasury and the Fed have seldom achieved. But the current consensus for growth could give President Bush the political Roto-Rooter he needs to clear out the conduit.

This problem didn't start on September 11th. U.S. banks have been closed for business lending for more than a year. The story reads a lot like the real-estate blowout of the early 1990s that ended with Resolution Trust Corp (RTC) auctions, except this time it was undisciplined technology investments that did us in. In the three years leading up to 2000, commercial banks loaned enormous sums of money to telecom, cable and technology companies to finance capital-spending programs. These loans weren't backed by assets, but were based on projections that all three sectors would have sales growth rates several times that of the overall economy for many years to come.

During the summer of 2000, it became clear that sales growth would not meet those heady projections. Instead of the 14% growth projected by analysts for telecom companies this year, for example, actual sales will shrink. Companies without revenues don't make interest payments. And so by the fall of 2000, OCC teams were forcing regional banks to downgrade loans and reduce business lending.

Here's the catch. The loans to technology companies were generally unrecoverable. The tech firms had spent the funds on current operating expenses or to purchase assets with lots of goodwill but little resale value. So the banks turned to the one place they could get money back: reducing the revolving credit facilities of their small business customers.

I got a personal glimpse of all this in October 2000, when a team of bankers visited our office to inform us their bank had decided to reduce the credit rating and cash-flow loans of one of the private companies we own, in preparation for a bank examiner audit the following week. New OCC requirements meant that our company's loan went from a "five" to a "six" on the bank's 10-point internal risk management system, which meant the company could no longer use its acquisition credit line. This caused the company to halt discussions with an acquisition target and to book the costs incurred up to that point as current expenses.

Other companies had it worse, with reduced revolving credit facilities and increased fees. Some companies, under pressure from their banks to raise equity capital, have been forced to sell control in the illiquid private equity market. Others have been forced into filing for bankruptcy protection or liquidation.

Deprived of working capital, U.S. companies have been trying to shrink their way to solvency, by reducing inventory, stretching vendors and laying off workers. This has created the sharpest drop in industrial output in 20 years.

Ironically, when the Fed became alarmed at the shrinking economy and began to cut interest rates in January, the bank examiners, who report to a different master, tightened further. The business loan market is far tighter today than it was then. Two years ago, banks were willing to lend a good company four to five times EBITDA (earnings before interest, taxes, depreciation and amortization). Today, banks quote a market of just over two times EBITDA, but money is not, in fact, available even at that lower level.

A further irony is that although banks have refused to lend to businesses, they were throwing money at the consumer through mortgage and equity credit lines because they can package and sell these loans in the asset-backed bond market. This produced a two-speed economy that left many companies unable to produce products or to ship orders for lack of working capital. Stimulating consumer spending won't solve this problem; we need a functioning bank market.

The last period of non-price credit rationing was the 1990-92 credit crunch. It caused tremendous damage to the economy and cost the first President Bush his re-election bid. It ended only after the RTC had finished its auctions and the property and banking markets had stabilized.

The lesson of that experience—that the economy is only as healthy as its balance sheet—is as true today as it was a decade ago. Unless the current Bush administration takes steps to restore bank lending to small businesses and heal the asset markets now, the economy will stay weak.

The White House can do three things to put the economy back on sound footing.

First, it should bring the Fed and the Comptroller of the Currency together to coordinate efforts to restore bank lending. This can be done very quickly and would not require new legislation.

Second, it should introduce legislation to transfer the regulation of federally chartered banks from the Treasury to the Fed, which would make monetary policy function more smoothly and prevent future credit-crunch situations.

Third, the White House should make it clear to Congressional leaders that the price for support of their huge spending projects is fast action on lower capital gains and dividend tax rates and further action to lower marginal income tax rates, all of which would increase asset market values and improve bank capital.

Forceful action to Roto-Rooter the business loan pipeline is one thing we can do to make the economy grow again.

## The Two-Cylinder Economy

Shortly later, I wrote the following article to explain why a credit crunch has a more powerful impact on the private companies that account for 55% of GDP and 100% of new jobs than it does on public companies. This analysis led me to shift my stock market bets entirely away from small-cap companies that get their money from banks to large-cap companies that get their money in the public markets, and which were benefiting from lower Fed funds rates. The article, written in early 2002, follows.

—

*Warning:* The following article uses terminology that may not be familiar to people under the age of 50. A *carburetor* is a device used in the early days of the automobile; cars don't have them anymore. Examples can still be seen on the classic movie channel in movies starring Steve McQueen or Burt Reynolds. Carburetors are the things that Marlon Brando and Elvis Presley were adjusting under the hood of their cars, that Humphrey Bogart was always fiddling with in *The African Queen,* and that Ross Perot was going to "get under the hood" and fix if he got to be President. Their function was to control the flow of gasoline into the cylinders of a motor. Your parents' car had one of them, cool cars had two—known as twin-carbs—and racecars had four. Twin carbs made your car use more gas, go faster, and make that cool sucking sound when you accelerated, like Sal Mineo's car in *Rebel Without a Cause.* This made your car a *babe magnet.* This was OK because gas was 29 cents per gallon and they hadn't invented OPEC yet.

In spite of the whining about the credit crunch I have been doing over the past couple of months in my *Wall Street Journal* editorials, there are signs the economy is beginning to recover. The big question now is whether the recovery will be slow or fast, and what that implies for the stock market. I believe it will be a two-speed recovery, with large, public companies growing rapidly and small, private companies still sucking air for lack of working capital. This implies a big year for the stock market and plenty of takeover activity, and says small-cap value stocks should beat large-cap growth stocks for the year. Here are the reasons why.

The early signs of growth are returning. I first saw it in early December when the CEO of one of our companies in the retail custom framed art business—$200 discretionary consumer purchases—told me he had just completed the two biggest weekends he'd had in a year. Another CEO saw daily sales jump 50% above November levels. A third said sales were above plan for the first time in months. Apparently, people had turned off CNN and gone back to their real day jobs—shopping. All this made the Christmas shopping season not as bad as retailers had feared.

A group of apparel industry CEOs told me in November that retailers had cancelled or reduced Christmas orders after 9/11 and were pushing unwanted or unsold inventory back onto manufacturers. Now the same retailers are starting to worry about stock-outs, not having what their customers want to buy. Orders for more products will soon follow.

The head of a major bank bond desk told me the high-yield market is starting to loosen up again, with investors showing interest in LBO credits again for the first time in ages. Liquidity is still scarce and the minimum size for a new issue is still $200 million, but it is improving. The yield curve is very steep, which shows that investors expect firming short-term rates next year. And the mutual funds are still holding a ton of cash.

The recovery will be quicker and stronger than most people are expecting, with the first measurable impact on growth appearing in the first quarter, as businesses stop drawing down inventories and reorder to fill their empty shelves.

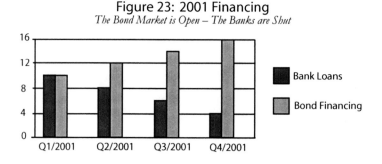

### Figure 23: 2001 Financing
*The Bond Market is Open – The Banks are Shut*

But there are some interesting things taking place below the GDP level that can make investors money. The monetary base is growing and interest rates are low. Large corporations are borrowing tons of low-cost money in the bond market. But the credit crunch is still alive and well for the small, private companies that make up the bulk of the economy. Commercial and industrial loans continue to fall as more regional banks pull out of middle-market cash flow lending. This guarantees we will have a two-speed recovery. Large, public companies that get their money in the public markets will resume healthy growth with increased profitability as early as the first quarter. Small, private companies that rely on their bank for working capital will continue to be liquidity-constrained.

This is great for the stock market. First, it will help keep interest rates down. We all know the Fed hates GDP growth. The two-speed recovery implies modest average GDP growth—GDP is overwhelmingly dominated by small companies—and no job growth. That should suppress the normal Federal Reserve knee-jerk response to growth, which is to tighten interest rates at the first sign of strength. Big companies, however, the ones that are listed in the stock market, will use their ample supply of cheap credit to grow faster than GDP. That means we should see strong reported earnings growth for S&P companies of 15-20% next year. And it means we will see a lot of M&A activity as larger companies, with low financing costs and big multiples, pick off smaller companies with good core assets, valuable brands and strong future prospects, but with values that have been depressed by tight liquidity and weak trailing performance. It will be a tough year for small private companies again.

The Federal Reserve is pursuing two monetary policies, not one. Like the driver of a racecar, when the Fed wants the economy to go faster they press on the accelerator by injecting reserves into the economy and reducing interest rates. They have been doing that for more than a year now, as evidenced by double-digit growth rates for the monetary base. This racecar, however, has two cylinders and twin carburetors. One cylinder of the economy—large, public companies—gets its fuel from the public markets in the form of commercial paper, bond, or stock issues. The other—small, private companies—gets its fuel from commercial banks as commercial and industrial loans. The Fed has been reducing interest rates, trying to make the economy go faster for more than a year, with absolutely no results. What's wrong?

The problem, as I wrote in the November 6th *Wall Street Journal*, is that one of our two carburetors is clogged. Bank regulators effectively shut down bank lending about a year ago when they recognized the severity of impending losses on bank loans to telecom and technology companies made during the previous three years. Since then, large banks' commercial and industrial loans have dropped by more than $60 billion.

The other carburetor is working fine. Cheap money is flowing to large, public companies in the form of massive bond refinancing activity and through high stock market multiples.

The reason GDP has not responded is that most business in America is small business.

The clogged carburetor problem has set up an interesting dilemma for the Fed and a related risk for investors. With the economy not responding to interest rate reductions all last year, the Fed was forced to press harder and harder on the accelerator. Because of this, the interest rates the public sees—Treasury bills, commercial paper, money market yields, bond yields—are now far lower than they would have had to be to produce today's anemic economic growth if both cylinders had been firing properly.

The risk for investors is today's high price-earnings multiples. As with a bond, the duration of a stock, which measures the sensitivity of its price to changes in interest rates, increases as interest rates fall. At today's interest rates, the duration of the S&P Industrials is 26, compared with 15 for the thirty-year Treasury bond. That makes stock prices exquisitely sensitive to cost of capital changes at current rate levels. A one percent, or one hundred basis point, increase in bond yields would reduce stock market multiples and prices by 26%.

Should the credit crunch suddenly end and private companies get access to the working capital they need to grow, the economy would take off like a rocket. That would cause the growth-haters at the Fed to push rates higher, resulting in a severe blow to the stock market.

Fortunately, this risk is unlikely for the next year. As my WSJ exchange with the Comptroller of the Currency shows, the bank regulators are not exactly wringing their hands over the credit crunch. And the weak leadership of Paul O'Neill at the Treasury suggests the White House is not likely to take aggressive steps to address the problem. That means the banking problem will likely be solved the old-fashioned way, by allowing bank capital ratios to gradually be restored by the investment profits that banks are raking in from the steep yield curve. That process takes 18-24 months. Until that happens, the Fed is likely to hold rates just where they are, which will provide a firm foundation for valuations in the stock market next year.

## Zero Inflation of What?

I wrote the following article in 1990 to question the Greenspan Fed's zealous devotion to controlling the Consumer Price Index (CPI), which measures the prices of haircuts and guitar lessons. Asset prices, not haircut prices, are what monetary policy should worry about. Unfortunately, the Bernanke Fed is still doing the same thing today with equally unimpressive results.

——

Zero inflation is a terrific idea. But inflation of what? Analytically, inflation is bad for an economy for the same reasons tax shelters are bad: it distorts investment choices. Inflation artificially subsidizes the real after-tax return on the ownership of tangible assets like cars, boats and houses, relative to the returns on bonds, stocks and other financial assets. Over time, this causes people to rebalance their portfolios toward the subsidized assets, diverting saving flows away from new tools and factories and toward hotels, office buildings and shopping centers.

But these analytical arguments only apply to physical, storable goods, not to services like haircuts and guitar lessons. It is for real goods prices that zero inflation is the right target.

Unfortunately, the Consumer Price Index, the deflator and most other price indexes used by the Fed to measure inflation are heavily weighted toward services. More than half of the CPI, for example, is accounted for by service prices. When goods and service prices diverge, as they are doing now, the Fed is misled into crippling the industrial economy in a misguided attempt to control service prices.

The problem is the productivity wedge between manufacturing and services. For most of the past decade, U.S. manufacturing has turned out an impressive productivity performance, with increases of more than 4% per year. The service sector, in contrast, has had a difficult time raising productivity at all. This discrepancy created the glut of manufactured goods that caused the much-maligned employment shift out of manufacturing and into service sector jobs during the 1980s. (A shift that, as William Baumol has pointed out, has taken place in every major industrial country in the world.) The productivity wedge, in turn, has created an inflation wedge: real goods prices are consistently falling by 4% to 5% per year relative to service prices.

For the first seven months of this year, for example, the goods component of the CPI only grew at a 1.8% annual rate. But service prices grew at 5.8%, so the CPI came in at 4.1%. The Fed, focusing on the CPI, thinks inflation is too high and is reluctant to provide sufficient credit for growth. It is possible, of course, for the Fed to tighten policy hard enough, for long enough, to bring the CPI inflation rate down to zero. Because of the productivity wedge, that can only be accomplished by a deflation of goods prices of 2% to 3% per year. But the stock of goods makes up the collateral of the nation's banking system. And deflating the banking system's collateral does not make for a healthy economy.

For manufacturing companies, this situation implies a chokingly high real interest rate. A steel company I visited last week, for example, had done a great job running their business during the past year. Real volume had risen by 5%. The price of the company's product, however, had fallen by 7% over that same year so dollar revenues fell by 2% for the year. But the company's interest obligations are not falling. The managers must therefore make their payments out of declining dollar revenues while inventory valuations, and therefore credit lines, are falling. For them, the real interest rate—the difference between the interest rate that they pay (10%) and the change in the price of their product (-7%)—is a staggering 17%. For many managers today, the effective real interest-rate is much higher than that, because they can't get capital at all.

What the Fed should be doing is targeting the long-term behavior of prices for goods, not services—not just those of newly produced goods, but those of goods in the resale markets as well, including real estate and commodities. And right now, those prices are either flat or falling. It is easy to see that the Resolution Trust Corp. workout, which will force the sale of hundreds of billions of dollars in real estate, is going to put downward pressure on the prices of those assets. That will, in turn, undermine the capital adequacy of the banking industry, of life insurance companies and of corporate owners of fixed assets. These balance sheet problems, and the regulators' response to them, have effectively paralyzed the financial system's ability to provide working capital to our businesses and have led to a steady slowing of the economy all year.

## Evidence From Main Street

I wrote the following analysis of the credit crunch in 2003.

—

One of the questions I always get from readers is how to tell the difference between restricted credit and a decline of lending due to falling loan demand. Both, of course, would result in shrinking bank loan numbers. How do we know that declining outstanding loans are not simply a reflection of the decline in inventories that always accompanies a recession?

There are two answers to the question. The first, and by far the best, answer is to actually observe interactions between bankers and their customers as they happen, exactly as Chekhov would have done. That would, however, require economists to actually learn something about a real business, meet its managers, and spend time there—a clear violation of the macroeconomist's Hippocratic Oath to remain in the ivory tower and wait for new data to arrive in the campus mail. For some reason, the economics fraternity is highly suspicious of evidence that does not arrive in the form of a time series from a government agency.

I have always found real experiences in businesses to be the best form of information. (That's why I have so many frequent flyer miles.) I have personally witnessed credit restriction in dozens of private companies. I know of no single professional in the private equity industry—the people best placed to see the daily interaction between private companies and their banks—who questions the dramatic tightening of credit availability.

In a real company, the best measure of credit availability is the amount of money a bank will lend a profitable business per dollar of EBIT, EBITDA, or some other measure of profitability. When credit tightens, that is the number that shrinks. Two years ago, a typical bank would lend a healthy company $3.50 for each dollar of cash profit it earned during the previous year. That way the company would have about three times the profit they needed to pay the interest on the loan—roughly ten percent of $3.50, or 35 cents.

Today, the same company with the same one dollar of profits would only be able to borrow $2.00. Business owners wanting to borrow money to invest in new plant and equipment or to finance payroll, inventories and receivables for growth have to trim their projects to fit the smaller appetites of the banks.

The real problem, however, is for companies who have already borrowed money and deployed the funds in new capital. When their banker announces they must bring their loan into line with the new market terms—and they do—the manager has no alternative but to raise cash by firing employees, leaning harder on customer collections, stretching vendors and scrapping new product launches. All shrink the economy.

## Secondary Markets and the Tech Rebound

The best way to know when an economy is starting to turn around is to keep tabs on resale prices in the secondary markets. Before eBay, we had to do that by calling a lot of resellers and junk dealers. Now it is a lot easier. This is as true today as it was when I wrote this article on tech equipment in 2003.

—

In my piece last week on Japanese deflation, I asserted that asset markets exert powerful effects on the real, or production, economy—the one we measure with GDP—through the junkyard effect. This is where sharp declines in secondary market prices undercut the sales efforts of primary producers, causing a virtual shutdown in production. This article describes the impact the junkyard effect has had on the technology sector over the past year and why the recovery in revenues will be sharper and quicker than most analysts believe.

Property developers know what I mean by the junkyard effect. About once every decade the Federal Reserve floods the market with liquidity or there is a new tax bill, and the prices of existing buildings spike up relative to construction costs. For two to three years, they work around the clock to build new factories, hotels, and shopping centers.

About once every decade the Federal Reserve turns off the liquidity tap and the prices of existing properties collapse far below construction costs. And for two to three years, the developers can't get any work at all.

The metals and other commodity markets go through the same feast or famine swing, as do the auto, appliance and furniture markets.

What do all these markets have in common? They are all markets where there are many years of already-produced output sitting in stockpiles. Such markets behave more like asset markets than product markets. Producers have about as much control over sales of new products as a tick riding on a dog.

Textbooks call it the business cycle, but there is nothing cyclical about it. It is caused by the interaction of the resale, or secondary markets—the junkyard—with the primary producers whose output we measure in GDP. In these industries, when the junkyard is having a clearance sale, you might as well go to the beach.

The only difference today is that the junkyard discounters have set up shop in the technology infrastructure and telecommunications equipment industries—the primary engines of U.S. growth over the past decade. Thanks to the misguided telecom legislation in 1996, aggressive banks, an eager junk bond market, a cooperative Fed and an army of day-traders, we experienced the phenomenal tech boom of the late 1990s. When the tide went out last year, the landscape was littered with bankrupt cable and telecom companies whose only recoverable assets were the routers, servers, and other IT equipment they had bought on the way up. The bang of the auctioneer's gavel was our first hint of the recession to come.

Here's how it works. Figure 24 shows the economics of an industry that produces a product that lasts for more than one GDP period, i.e., one with a depreciation rate less than 100% per year. For the U.S., this would include all homes, factories, office buildings, capital goods, and consumer durable goods.

## Figure 24: An Equipment Market

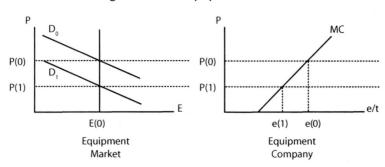

Equipment Market | Equipment Company

The left-hand chart depicts the asset (secondary) market. There is an existing stock of equipment, $E(0)$, which is represented by an essentially vertical supply curve. Supply does not depend on price; it depends on history, because any unit that still exists must be owned by somebody, regardless of price. This stockpile of existing equipment will grow over time as we produce new units of equipment (right-hand chart), and will shrink over time as the existing equipment depreciates at a rate equal to the inverse of the useful lifespan, or duration of the equipment.

The demand to hold the existing equipment depends on price, as well as on other things, and slopes downward in the normal way. The inherited stockpile $E(0)$ and initial demand $D(0)$ result in asset market equilibrium at a secondary market price of $P(0)$.

The right-hand chart shows the economics of an individual producer of equipment, such as Cisco, Nortel, or Sun, in the technology equipment industry. Its horizontal axis measures the flow of production measured in new equipment units per year. The company increases production as long as the price at which it can sell the product exceeds the Marginal Cost of production, shown as the upward sloping MC curve in Figure 24.

At price P(0), the equipment maker produces and sells at a rate of e(0) units per year. This is the number that will be measured in the GDP accounts.

I realize that depicting the demand for firm output as horizontal is stretching the analogy a bit. In the real world, each producer will have at least some control over its customers. But the main point, that there is a huge secondary market for the same products where customers can go if they find the price compelling, still holds.

If there is a sudden, sharp drop in demand in the secondary markets—caused, for example, by a reduction in credit availability due to tight Fed policy—the secondary market price will fall to P(1), the price at which customers are again willing to own the stock of existing products. If the equipment maker is able to reduce its price quickly enough through the use of discounts, it will sell e(1) units at the new price P(1). If it does not have business practices in place that allow it to quickly change prices, however, and holds its price at P(0), it will not sell any product at all. Its customers can get all the product they want at the junk dealer.

Both the decline in price and the decline in output contribute to lower revenues and a drop in measured GDP. Resale activity is not picked up in the GDP accounts at all.

Most markets with large existing stockpiles of output have developed elaborate mechanisms to allow new product prices to quickly adapt to changing secondary market conditions or to reduce headcount through layoffs so factories can remain open during downturns. These include finance cost buy-downs in real estate, subsidized financing costs, trade-in allowances, rebates in autos, and buy-now-pay-later plans in appliances, furniture and other consumer durables. Relatively new industries such as technology equipment, however, that have grown rapidly in the past decade have not yet had time to develop these mechanisms. They have born the brunt of the recent slowdown.

### Figure 25: 2002 IT Equipment Sales
*(billions of dollars)*

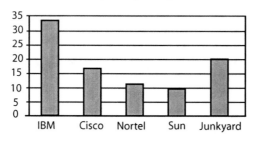

Figure 25 reproduces estimates of 2002 IT equipment sales from a February 4, 2002 *Fortune* article titled "Cisco's Worst Nightmare." The article described the tidal wave of "unboxed inventory" being sold in bankruptcy auctions for pennies on the dollar of original cost. The buyers are the more than 2,000 resellers—junkyard dealers—who, in turn, sell the product to companies who would otherwise buy from original equipment makers.

As the chart shows, the junkyards have the #2 market share in the U.S., with devastating effects on profit margins for the industry—in spite of aggressive efforts on the part of producers to shut the secondary market down by refusing to deliver software updates and refusing to honor warranty claims on products bought in the secondary market. This $20 billion in sales alone is enough to reduce GDP by 20 basis points for the year without even considering the dampening effects on prices and margins at the primary producers.

Every company that produces a durable product is competing more with its own used product than with its rival across town. In the case of autos, for example, there are more than ten used cars in driveways for every new car that will be produced this year. Computers, technology infrastructure and telecom equipment makers are no different.

But there is good news in this story, too. Watch out for the whipsaw effect when the secondary markets firm, as they always do. The Federal Reserve has been attempting to re-inflate the economy for more than a year now, with dramatic increases in the monetary base and reductions in interest rates. The economy is starting to grow. And my own personal contacts at used equipment resellers are telling me they are starting to have stock-outs of selected products.

When the junkyard doesn't have the router you need, you are going to have to buy it from Cisco again. When that happens, pricing will firm and we will see a sharp rebound in both sales and margins in the industry.

# 8

# Competing for Capital

*Last thing I remember, I was running for the door.*
*I had to find the passage back to the place I was before.*
*'Relax,' said the night man, we are programmed to receive.*
*You can check out any time you like but you can never leave.*

—The Eagles, "Hotel California"

Some governments get it. Some don't. Countries are not competing for jobs today; they are competing for capital. Access to capital—modern tools, education, training, technology and working capital—is what makes workers productive.

## Capital Makes Paychecks Possible

Not so long ago, national governments were able to hold capital owners hostage and count the capital within their borders as national assets to do with as they pleased. Capital was expensive to move from one country to another. Moving capital was slow, at the speed of cargo ships—easy for governments to see, tax and regulate.

No longer. Modern communications networks and efficient capital markets have changed the rules of the game. Today, global investors can move capital from any country in the world to any country in the world, whenever they please. These capital movements occur at the speed of light over fiber-optic networks at virtually no cost to investors. They are virtually invisible to governments.

Governments who ignore these changes in the mobility of capital do so at the peril of their workers' paychecks.

## China Gets It

I have traveled to China a lot in recent years. I have spent lots of time in Beijing with government officials who definitely get it. They are taking steps to make China a destination resort for capital. China's leaders realize that the only way to deliver continued high economic growth without further fouling the air and water or running out of energy is to focus on IT, communications and financial services. They are adopting policies to convince foreign investors to relocate their R&D operations in China with tax breaks, development funds and other policies. China's new policy mantra is 'Innovation and Entrepreneurship'—and they are doing the things necessary to deliver on that promise.

Here are recent manifestations of China's enthusiasm for attracting capital to grow. In a one week period, I spoke at: 1) a venture capital forum in Haidian (Beijing's Silicon Valley), where the government announced a new fund to attract foreign capital, 2) the opening of a new finance school in Xicheng, Beijing's financial district, to train people to be employed by the foreign banks, insurance companies, investment banks and investment managers who will open up shop after China completes its obligation to open its capital markets, and 3) the International Financial Forum, which included talks by top Chinese officials on the importance of attracting foreign capital and a discussion of a new special enterprise zone in Tientsin to conduct an experiment on currency convertibility—a crucial issue for foreign investors.

During that same week, the Chinese government announced major revisions to its tax rebate system for exports. These changes reduced rebates (discouraged investment) in coal, gas, steel, non-ferrous metals, glass, cement, textiles, cigarette lighters, wooden products and other natural resources, but increased rebates (encouraged investment) in biotech, pharmaceuticals and telecommunications. And I had dinner with the executive producer of China's hit TV show *Win in China*, where 120,000 young entrepreneurs across China are competing to win 10 million RMB ($1.2 million) in venture capital financing for their business plan.

## U.S. Policy Makers Don't Get It—Yet

I have also spent time with leaders who definitely do not get it. Unfortunately, they are our leaders. In a world where countries are scrambling to attract capital—especially high-tech capital—Congress is too concerned with lobby groups, earmarked expenditures and elections to worry about attracting and holding capital. Like Nero, they are fiddling while Rome burns, wasting their time fighting over non-issues like so-called network neutrality and deciding which snouts will enjoy the $7.3 billion Universal Service Fund trough instead of passing the communications legislation overhaul we need to drive investment and productivity higher.

Meanwhile, company after company is moving R&D facilities offshore—the share of U.S. companies in the global telecom equipment market has fallen from 40% to 20% in the past 5 years.

## Technology

I wrote the following piece about the importance of technology after the dot-com bust.

—

Investors and managers who learned their trade since 1981 have a prominent weakness in their toolkit. They think they have had over 20 years of experience. In fact, they have had the same one-year of experience twenty times. There has only been one story since 1981, the incredible shift of wealth from real to financial assets caused by lower inflation and tax rates. Until recently, if you got that right, nothing else mattered.

The economy has moved on to a new story. Today, the driving force in the economy is technological change. This is no accident—the two are directly linked. The aftermath of the Reagan era was a low inflation, low interest rate environment that set up the incentives that made the economy ripe for innovation. This means that investors, managers and policy makers must make decisions differently. The technology boom is the result of those decisions.

In late 1980, inflation was 15% and the top marginal tax rate was 70% on earned income. Investors knew you made money by owning real estate and that you kept your financial assets in the money market, where rates were more than 20%. Managers indexed their prices and wages, avoided long-term contracts with their customers, and refused to do capital spending on all but the quickest payout projects.

In the early days of the Reagan administration, I wrote articles arguing that lower inflation and tax rates would lead to massive rebalancing of investors' portfolios, systematically driving the prices of real assets down and the prices of financial assets up, reducing interest rates. This would be true regardless of budget deficit and savings behavior.

Over the past 20-plus years, this story has dominated the U.S. economic landscape. Inflation has declined from double-digit levels to the 1-3% range we see in most western economies today. Hard asset producers and heavy industry have lived through a wrenching restructuring. Managers learned how to use less capital to run their businesses by switching to Just-In-Time (JIT) Inventory Management and flow manufacturing methods. Long-term interest rates fell by two-thirds from 15% to 5%. As a result, stock market valuations have soared to record levels.

These transitory macro effects are now pretty well understood. The micro effects of low inflation are not as easy to see but they are much more important, because they have permanently altered our expectations, in the sense of Dickens, of an unearned legacy. In 1980, a 40-year-old person with a job and a home could reasonably expect his income to increase by 10% per year for the rest of his working life, simply due to indexed wages. And he could expect the value of his $100,000 house to increase by 10%, or $10,000, the following year, and so on. At the point of his retirement at age 65, he would be earning ten times as much in wages and salary per year and his (now older) house would be worth more than a million dollars.

In 1980, people were awash in a sea of expected future income. One by one, since 1980, disinflation has erased these sources of income. Like a neutron bomb, it has killed the income streams but left the people standing, wondering how they are going to get by in future years. This systematic drying-up of income sources has made future dollars—the price of a long-dated zero coupon bond—very expensive, and interest rates very low.

This has had, and will continue to have, profound effects on people's lives. The most visible micro effect of the past 25 years is that the steady decline of interest rates and steady increase in stock market valuations have made total returns in the stock market huge, both relative to history and in relation to the underlying returns on the companies themselves. Everyone wants to be an investment banker or a stock market investor, and a restructuring expert rather than an efficient operator. But underlying those huge total returns is a growing paucity of companies with sustainable growing cash profits. After all, in an economy with 2% inflation and 3% growth, like the U.S. in recent years, we would expect operating profits to rise at only 5% a year.

In this world of scarce future income streams, anyone who can create a new one from scratch by building a company with demonstrated growth prospects will be anointed an instant paper millionaire by a hungry IPO market. In this world of hungry young people, the best and brightest will migrate into operating, engineering and entrepreneurial jobs, minting future income from their own sweat and creative efforts. That is what is happening today in Silicon Valley.

This phenomenon has happened before. It is no accident that the introduction of railroads, the telegraph, electricity and telephones all took place after a fifty-year period of declining prices, and wages and interest rates. Entrepreneurs are more likely to make the long duration investments required in start-ups when inflation and interest rates are low and visibility into the future is high.

And like previous episodes of major technological change, we had our bubble—this time in the prices of the dot-com stocks. The technology sector as a whole was vastly overvalued. But within that sector there are undervalued companies that will dominate the economy for the next hundred years. This is the natural order of things. We once had hundreds of automobile companies and dozens of railroads. Now we can count each on one hand. How many ISP's will have survived once the dust has settled?

The technology companies are just the visible tip of the iceberg. The real, lasting benefits of today's technology boom will be enjoyed by relatively simple companies. The Internet revolution is essentially a way of taking the time out of doing business. This temporal-suction device, by allowing companies to complete the same work in less time, allows them do more work in a day, week or year, i.e., it increases productivity and economic activity. At the macro level, this raises growth rates and lowers inflation.

For investors, this analysis implies times will be tougher. The big, easy gains in both the stock and bond market since 1982 have been driven by falling interest rates and rising multiples. Big returns in the future will be earned by identifying the companies that produce growing profits for their owners. That requires serious work and knowledge of companies, products, technologies and managers.

For managers, this means the restructuring, re-engineering mindset of the '90s won't work. They must focus instead on top-line growth, research and development, marketing and e-commerce. The technology revolution creates tremendous incentives to find ways to sell more products, and gives them the tools to do so. Every company I know, large or small, has an e-commerce initiative now underway.

For the government, the key question is what the Fed should do to handle bubbles without interfering with innovation. Federal tax policy should give small companies the incentives to experiment with new technologies and should keep capital gains tax rates as low as possible to encourage value-creating investments. And it should not allow state and local governments to derail the Internet growth train by taxing e-commerce sales.

## Tax Technology—Tax Growth

A recent report said that China was repealing some of the tax incentives they had put in place to attract capital. Like most stories that come out, the story is about half right. The Chinese authorities have announced a series of tax changes that they refer to as "equalizing" the tax rates paid by domestic and foreign firms doing the same work. Of course with taxes, the devil is always in the details, so broad statements are not very useful for real businesses.

It's the story under the story that is interesting to me. China's growth and foreign direct investment (FDI) over the past 20 years has been heavily dependent on manufacturing. As a result, manufacturing makes up a larger share of Chinese GDP than any other major country.

By one account, half the manufacturing capacity in the world is in China. That has made a tremendous impact on the lives of Chinese people; average incomes have roughly quadrupled since the reforms began almost 30 years ago. But the growth in manufacturing has also led to worsening air and water quality, a widening rural-urban income gap and worries over the security of future energy supplies.

China's government has decided to attack the problems head-on by pushing energy conservation. They are increasing energy supplies and investing heavily in renewable energy projects. Both measures are important, but they only buy time. The real answer lies in their shift of focus from manufacturing to technology to drive growth.

This is where the tax changes come into the argument. China has increased taxes on steel and other heavy manufacturing industries, but has lowered taxes on information and communications technology companies. They are also aggressively courting tech companies to relocate R&D facilities to China with tax breaks and other subsidies. The biggest carrot of all is China's massive investments in math and science education and aggressive English language education programs.

These are exactly the policies we should be pursuing in the United States. Instead, our Congress couldn't even pass the telecom reform bill that would have triggered billions of dollars in new investment. They failed to pass video franchise legislation that would have allowed a massive rollout of optical fiber to homes. And they flirted with price controls to protect the current market cap of the big Internet providers under the misleading heading of "net neutrality." It was a shameful year for U.S. technology policy.

Instead of competing for high-tech capital, we tax and regulate it out of the country—U.S. companies bear a 22% excess overhead burden compared with overseas competitors. And we tax communications services—the central nervous system of the economy—as if it were a sin to talk with your customer or supplier, or even your family, on the phone. Depending on where you live in America, between 15-30% of your wireless phone bill goes to excise taxes.

Meanwhile in Shanghai, a pilot project was recently announced to provide 4G mobile services that would allow selected customers to transmit content at speeds greater than enjoyed by most fiber optic users in the United States.

We need to wise up and do the things now to make our technology companies believe they should build their businesses here. We don't have a lot of time to waste.

## The Broadband Race

A reader recently asked me about the role of communications technology in our global competitiveness:

I have a question for you concerning the future of broadband in the U.S. With Verizon and AT&T rolling out FiOS and U-verse broadband nationwide, do you not think that it's just a matter of time before we move up the ladder with respect to our 16th rank worldwide? Both companies are bypassing Federal legislation flaws and proceeding with individual state legislation for relief. I understand this will slow the process but perhaps at the same time we will reach our goals.

I wish that were true. U.S. companies are making substantial investments in new high-speed networks, but they are doing it in the face of regulatory, tax and legal burdens that would make me hesitant to approve the investments were I a director.

State legislatures have behaved more responsibly than the U.S. Congress, and several have passed legislation speeding new entry into video services. We should send the state legislators to Washington so they can fix the problem.

There is an old joke about two boys who come upon a bear while walking in the forest. "Let's get out of here," said the first boy. "Wait a minute, while I put on my sneakers," said the second. Boy #1 responded, "You're not going to outrun that bear just because you have sneakers on." Boy #2: "I don't have to outrun the bear. I just have to outrun you."

Competition always works that way—you just have to beat the other guy. Unfortunately, in this case, the other guy is investing his brains out both by building massive fiber-optic networks and by building new universities to train young people how to design the next technologies.

Here's an example. A story from the *Shanghai Daily* with the following headline, *China's 4G wireless launch leapfrogs 3G*, reported on the progress of a group of 10 Chinese companies that was field-testing a new wireless system that allows data transmission at up to 100 megabytes per second, several times faster than current technology.

As Chief Advisor to the Governor of Haidian—China's Silicon Valley in Beijing—I get a close look at these companies. As an Honorary Professor at the Chinese Academy of Sciences, I get to see the quality of basic research. Both are extremely impressive.

We're ahead of the bear—for now. But the bear is hungry. We'd better put on those sneakers soon.

## How the Dividend Tax Cut Increased Growth

As my old friends know, I am a big fan of making sure you distinguish between asset markets and flow markets when thinking about the economy. The reason is pretty simple. The GDP number is chump change in comparison with our asset markets.[1]

Bottom line: if a policy does not impact the asset markets, it does not matter. This is important because almost all of what passes for macroeconomic analysis today is simply descriptions of who is spending how much money in the GDP accounts. That analysis leads these thinkers to make big mistakes, which gives us great opportunities to make money.

I developed the following analysis of the way a reduction in tax rates impacts both the asset markets and growth by changing the rate of capital accumulation. I remember first drawing the graphs on a train on my way to make an asset allocation presentation to Dale Frey, John Myers and their portfolio managers at the GE pension fund. Presenting material to Dale always scared me into my best work. Dale is a very smart and gracious man, but he is very quick to spot the weak point in an argument.

---

[1] Some people ask whether GDP determines asset markets or the other way around. This is no different than asking whether the earth orbits the sun or the other way around. Most people know the sun is the big dog in this story and therefore think the earth orbits the sun. Actually, this is not true. (It would only be true if the earth had zero mass.) In fact, both the sun and the earth orbit the center of mass of the sun-earth system—it is because the sun has such a large mass that this point is inside (but not at the center of) the sun.

Take a look at Figure 26. In this diagram, the graph on the upper left represents the asset market in which the price $P$ of the existing capital stock, $K$, is determined.

## Figure 26: Capital Goods Market

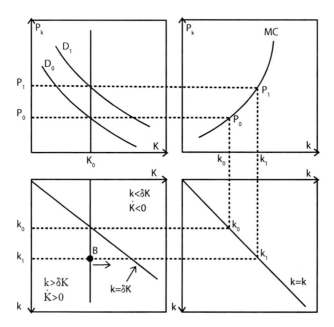

The graph on the upper right represents the new capital goods (flow) market in which the price of an existing machine, or other unit of capital, interacts with the marginal costs of machine manufacturers to determine the number of machines that will be built. We denote this value by lower-case $k$.

The lower right graph is simply a device for bringing big $K$ and little $k$ together on the same graph, which I have placed in the lower left. That is where all the action takes place.

In the graph on the upper left, a reduction in tax rates increases the demand to hold the existing stock of capital goods, which drives the price up from $P_0$ to $P_1$.

In the new machine market in the upper right graph, the higher machine price results in more machines being built per year, $k(1)$, than was the case at higher tax rates.

Now the hard part. The graph in the lower left is a phase diagram, a concept we can use to help think about dynamic change over time. The critical concept is the stationary state line descending from the origin downward and to the right. That line represents combinations of $K(t)$ and $k(t)$ that leave the existing capital stock unchanged. This will happen when the construction of new machines, $k(t)$ is just big enough to replace the number of machines that have worn out that year through depreciation. I have assumed that existing machines depreciate by delta ($\delta$) percent each year. For example, if a machine lasts 14 years, then delta ($\delta$) would be 7% per year.

Assume we start at $K(0)$ and $k(0)$, which is a point on the line described above, i.e., we start in a situation where the capital stock is neither growing nor shrinking. I can do this—it is my chart!

Now lower the tax rate on capital income. The higher demand in the upper left graph increases the price to $P(1)$, which increases machine production in the upper right to $k(1)$. But at $k(1)$, point B on the graph, we are building more machines than needed to replace the ones wearing out. Therefore, the capital stock is growing. A little thought will show you that all the points downward and to the left of the line in the lower left graph represent situations of a growing capital stock. In fact, the distance from the line even indicates how fast it is increasing. Conversely, all points to the right of the line represent a shrinking capital stock. In our scenario, the capital stock will continue to grow until machine production and depreciation are once again equal and the capital stock comes to rest at a higher level in a new stationary state.[2]

A drop in tax rates on capital income will make an initial spike in machine prices but, over time, the growing capital stock will mitigate some of the price pressure, which means the initial burst of activity, and possibly of price, are likely to moderate somewhat over time. To an information theorist, the initial spike in price is a way of amplifying the initial information signal that capital is now scarce, in order to get everybody's attention so that they get to work and build more capital goods.

So tax-cut induced capital inflation is largely a one-time event, but leads to a permanently higher capital stock. This leads to permanent increases in productivity and incomes, and barring any subsequent change in monetary policy, a permanently lower price level.

This story would play out in reverse if there were a sudden increase in tax rates. The result would be a drop in capital goods prices, reduced investment, a shrinking capital stock, and slower productivity and income growth.

## Why a Dividend Tax Cut Makes Sense

I wrote the following analysis of the impact of a dividend tax cut on the stock market in December, 2002, at the request of the White House in the weeks before they announced the tax cuts.

—

Dividends are currently taxed twice, once at the corporate level, then again at the investor level, which makes it hard to get a dollar of profit into an investor's pocket. Consider, as an illustration, XYZ

---

[2]  Geek note: Ludwig von Mises would have referred to such a point as an evenly rotating economy. Richard Dawkins and other ethologists and system theorists would call it ESS, or evolutionary stable system. It is not a point of equilibrium in the thermodynamic sense of a low energy state, but is held at a fixed distance from equilibrium by the flow of energy provided by the production of new capital goods.

Corporation. At current tax rates, XYZ has to earn $2.51 in pretax profits to put $1.00 of dividends in its shareholders' pockets.

Out of the $2.51 of pretax profits, it pays $0.88 (35% of pretax profits) in corporate income taxes to the IRS, leaving $1.63 in after-tax profits. If it pays that $1.63 to investors as a dividend, the investor receiving that dividend pays an additional $0.63 (38.6% of dividend income at the top marginal rate) to the IRS, leaving exactly $1.00 in his pocket.

Double taxation makes dividends an extremely leaky and inefficient bucket for carrying profits from the corporation to the investor. Overall, $1.51 (60%) of XYZ's original $2.51 has gone to pay taxes; only $1.00 (40%) found its way to the investor. In comparison, both interest payments and capital gains are more efficient channels for paying profits to investors. It would cost XYZ only $1.63 in interest payments to put a dollar of after-tax income in investors' pockets, since interest is deducted as an expense at the corporate level. Better still, XYZ could put the same after-tax dollar in investors' pockets by delivering only $1.25 in the form of capital gains—tax free to the corporation; 20% tax rate to the individual—by reinvesting profits to generate growth or by "investing" its after-tax profits in stock buybacks.

Not surprisingly, corporate managers have figured this out; paying dividends has gone out of style. Only 20.8% of public companies paid dividends in 1999, down from 66.5% as recently as 1978. Those that do pay dividends are paying out a lower share of profits or using stock buybacks in their place.

Double-taxation of dividend income has given rise to serious inefficiencies in capital markets. It has diverted capital away from business ventures that produce reliable, large and growing free cash flow streams for their owners in favor of companies that produce no profit but offer a hope of future capital gain. This distortion of managerial incentives was a material contributor to the excesses of the stock market boom in the late 1990s and the severity of the subsequent correction. It also created the presumption in the minds of many managers that they should avoid paying profits to investors, which contributed to the governance scandals that were exposed by declining equity values in the past few years.

Cutting the dividend tax rate at the investor level to zero would promote more efficient use of capital among competing uses by removing the existing distortion among the after-tax returns that guide investor behavior. Here's how it would work.

### How a Lower Dividend Tax Rate Affects Stock Prices

The way to understand the dividend tax cut is to focus on the economy's capital accounts, by analyzing the effects of changes in the dividend tax rate on relative asset demands, and therefore on asset prices and investment spending. Start with the example of a zero-growth company XYZ, discussed above, that has no debt and pays out 100% of its after-tax profits as dividends. Last year, the company paid shareholders a dividend of $1.63 per share. Shareholders paid 38.6% (their marginal income tax rate) of the dividend, or $0.63, to the IRS and put the remaining $1.00 in their pockets. XYZ's stock price is $20 per share. Shareholders earned a 5% after-tax return on their investment—$1.00/$20.00—which is exactly equal to the after-tax return on all other assets.

I discussed thermodynamics in Chapter 6, and the same principles apply here. If you put a hot object and a cold object into contact, heat will flow from the hot to the cold object until they reach thermal equilibrium where there is no temperature difference. You can try this yourself by placing a steaming hot dog and an icy cold can of soda into your child's lunch pail in the morning and ask them to report what they find when they open it to eat lunch. Your child may learn some physics. Even better, they may start making their own lunch.

If you put two objects together that are the same temperature, however, nothing will happen. Physicists call this situation thermal equilibrium.

This principle works in asset markets just as well as it does in lunch pails; only in economics we call it arbitrage and we refer to thermal equilibrium as portfolio balance. Unlike heat, however, money runs uphill, from low after-tax return to high after-tax return investments. Just like in physics, asset markets reach thermal equilibrium when after-tax returns are equal.

Our XYZ company example, above, is in thermal equilibrium because all assets have the same 5% after-tax return. There is no opportunity for investors to improve their net worth position by trading one asset for another. Regardless of what they own, they will earn 5% after-tax.

The dividend tax cut changes all that. Assume the government passes a law that makes XYZ dividends tax-free. (A good lobbyist will do that.) The company still pays the same dividend to the investor, but now the investor gets to pocket the entire $1.63.

Now the investor earns \$1.63/20.00 = 8.15% on his investment after taxes. This is far better than the 5% investors are earning on other investments. This metaphorical temperature differential means that asset markets are no longer in thermal equilibrium. An investor can improve his position by selling one of his 5% assets and using the proceeds to buy XYZ stock. As all investors try to do so—they all have the same information—they will run into a traffic jam. They will all try to sell 5% assets to people who are trying to do the same thing, and will all try to buy XYZ stock from people who are also trying to buy XYZ shares. In this situation, we know one thing for sure; the price of XYZ shares will go up.

How much? If the market capitalization of XYZ is small compared with the market, so that we can ignore the effects on other asset prices, the price of XYZ will rise until after tax returns are again equal and thermal equilibrium has been reestablished. This will happen when the price of XYZ has risen to \$32.60, at which price its owners will earn an after-tax return of \$1.63/\$32.60 = 5% on their capital.

Where did the extra value come from? It is the present value of the cash flow stream that has been diverted from the IRS to investors.

Cutting the dividend tax rate from 38.6% to zero has increased the Intrinsic Value of XYZ stock from \$20 to \$32.60, an increase of 63%, which equals the ratio of (1 − old tax rate) and (1 − new tax rate).

Analytically, we can describe this as a decline in XYZ's cost of equity capital, the return it must pay investors to remain competitive with other uses for their capital. A decline in the cost of capital increases equity values as a multiple of current after-tax profits.

## Taxing Capital

The dividend tax cut will raise the after-tax return on dividend paying assets above that on all other assets. The resulting thermal disequilibrium will lead investors to rebalance portfolios, driving dividend paying asset prices up relative to other assets.

Conceptually, a dividend tax cut would impact stock prices in two phases. Initially, it would work by raising the after-tax return on dividend paying assets above that on all other assets. The resulting thermal disequilibrium, characterized by an unsustainable gap between after-tax returns, would lead investors to individually attempt to rebalance their portfolios, selling non-dividend paying assets to buy dividend paying assets.

Collectively, these attempts would drive the prices of dividend paying assets up relative to all other assets, which would reduce the after-tax return gap until returns were driven back in line. These price changes would increase the market value of equities, as well as the net worth of investors.

A reduction of the dividend tax rate from 38.6% to 0%, for example, would increase the Intrinsic Value of the S&P 900 by 8.5% and increase investors' net worth by $799 billion. A reduction of the dividend tax rate from 38.6% to 20% would increase the Intrinsic Value of the S&P 900 by 5.1% and increase investors' net worth by $481 billion.

## Table 1: Impact of 0% Dividend Tax Rate on Stock Prices

| Sector | Pre-Cut Cost of Equity | Dividend Payout (2001) | Post-Cut Cost of Equity | Cost of Equity Impact | Equity Capital Ratio | Cost of Capital Impact | Cost of Capital Sensitivity | Stock Price Impact | Pre-Cut Market Cap $B | Market Cap Impact $B |
|---|---|---|---|---|---|---|---|---|---|---|
| Consumer Discretionary | 7.1% | 52.0% | 5.7% | -1.4% | 42.5% | -0.6% | 25.4% | 15.5% | $1,304 | $202 |
| Consumer Staples | 7.4% | 45.2% | 6.1% | -1.3% | 43.3% | -0.6% | 18.8% | 10.5% | $844 | $88 |
| Industrials | 7.2% | 81.3% | 4.9% | -2.3% | 43.2% | -1.0% | 21.7% | 21.2% | $1,060 | $225 |
| Utilities | 7.7% | 56.0% | 6.0% | -1.7% | 33.7% | -0.6% | 22.9% | 12.7% | $244 | $31 |
| Materials | 7.4% | 115.3% | 4.1% | -3.3% | 44.0% | -1.5% | 16.0% | 23.3% | $263 | $61 |
| HealthCare | 7.2% | 33.2% | 6.3% | -0.9% | 46.9% | -0.4% | 18.3% | 7.9% | $1,360 | $108 |
| Information Technology | 7.0% | 12.8% | 6.7% | -0.3% | 65.7% | -0.2% | 23.6% | 5.4% | $1,482 | $80 |
| Financials | 7.3% | 47.0% | 6.0% | -1.3% | 11.9% | -0.2% | 29.7% | 4.7% | $1,904 | $89 |
| Energy | 7.4% | 37.1% | 6.3% | -1.1% | 59.5% | -0.6% | 19.0% | 11.9% | $525 | $63 |
| Telecommunications | 7.3% | 117.4% | 4.0% | -3.3% | 48.1% | -1.6% | 20.9% | 33.4% | $394 | $132 |
| S&P 900 | 7.2% | 52.9% | 5.8% | -1.5% | 27.2% | -0.4% | 21.2% | 8.5% | $9,381 | $799 |

## Table 2: Impact of 20% Dividend Tax Rate on Stock Prices

| Sector | Pre-Cut Cost of Equity | Dividend Payout (2001) | Post-Cut Cost of Equity | Cost of Equity Impact | Equity Capital Ratio | Cost of Capital Impact | Cost of Capital Sensitivity | Stock Price Impact | Pre-Cut Market Cap $B | Market Cap Impact $B |
|---|---|---|---|---|---|---|---|---|---|---|
| Consumer Discretionary | 7.1% | 52.0% | 6.3% | -0.9% | 42.5% | -0.4% | 25.4% | 9.3% | $1,304 | $121 |
| Consumer Staples | 7.4% | 45.2% | 6.6% | -0.8% | 43.3% | -0.3% | 18.8% | 6.3% | $844 | $53 |
| Industrials | 7.2% | 81.3% | 5.8% | -1.4% | 43.2% | -0.6% | 21.7% | 12.8% | $1,060 | $135 |
| Utilities | 7.7% | 56.0% | 6.7% | -1.0% | 33.7% | -0.3% | 22.9% | 7.7% | $244 | $19 |
| Materials | 7.4% | 115.3% | 5.4% | -2.0% | 44.0% | -0.9% | 16.0% | 14.1% | $263 | $37 |
| HealthCare | 7.2% | 33.2% | 6.6% | -0.6% | 46.9% | -0.3% | 18.3% | 4.8% | $1,360 | $65 |
| Information Technology | 7.0% | 12.8% | 6.8% | -0.2% | 65.7% | -0.1% | 23.6% | 3.2% | $1,482 | $48 |
| Financials | 7.3% | 47.0% | 6.5% | -0.8% | 11.9% | -0.1% | 29.7% | 2.8% | $1,904 | $54 |
| Energy | 7.4% | 37.1% | 6.7% | -0.6% | 59.5% | -0.4% | 19.0% | 7.2% | $525 | $38 |
| Telecommunications | 7.3% | 117.4% | 5.3% | -2.0% | 48.1% | -1.0% | 20.9% | 20.1% | $394 | $79 |
| S&P 900 | 7.2% | 52.9% | 6.3% | -0.9% | 27.2% | -0.2% | 21.2% | 5.1% | $9,381 | $481 |

Effects vary widely by sector, as shown above in Table 1 for the 0% dividend tax rate, and Table 2 for the 20% dividend tax rate. The biggest effects will occur in sectors with high dividend payout ratios and no debt. In the Telecommunications sector, for example, the reduction to a 0% dividend tax rate would increase equity value by 33.4%; the reduction to a 20% dividend tax rate would increase equity value by 20.1%.

A second round of potentially larger stock price increases will follow these initial effects as managers alter company strategies to take advantage of the new tax regime. One-time special dividends to distribute excess cash, increased payout ratios and issuing new shares to reduce debt will all increase value. These opportunities, which are concentrated in sectors with low payout ratios, like Information Technology, could be huge. Raising the dividend payout ratio in the Information Technology sector to 100%, for example, would increase equity values by 42.1% in the case of a 0% dividend tax rate.

I believe that the Bush dividend tax cut would be the biggest event to hit the asset markets since the 1981 Reagan tax cuts. It will have a huge impact on asset prices, interest rates, growth, and the dollar. It will create a host of opportunities for investors to make money. It will also create a wave of restructuring, recapitalization and acquisition events among U.S. companies.

### Figure 27: Stock Price Impact of a 0% Dividend Tax Rate

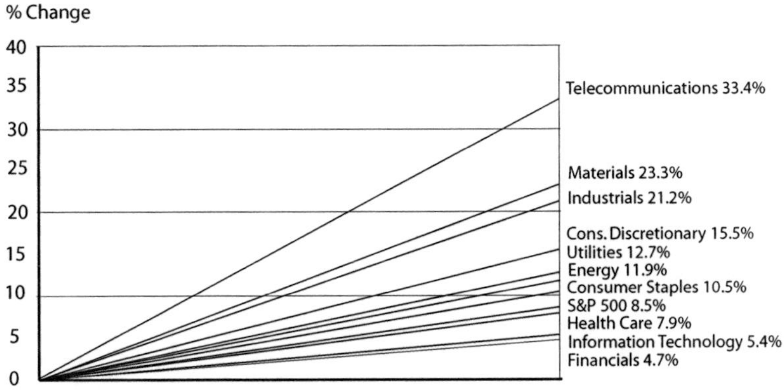

% Change

Telecommunications 33.4%

Materials 23.3%
Industrials 21.2%

Cons. Discretionary 15.5%
Utilities 12.7%
Energy 11.9%
Consumer Staples 10.5%
S&P 500 8.5%
Health Care 7.9%
Information Technology 5.4%
Financials 4.7%

*Manager Response: Restructuring and Refinancing*

Astute managers will soon learn that companies that take advantage of the new, lower, tax rates will have lower capital costs and become tougher competitors than others. Over time, they will adapt their business practices to the new tax regime. The irony is that the sectors, industries and companies that will initially benefit most from a lower dividend tax rate will have the least flexibility to improve their value, while those that initially benefit the least have the most to gain by changing behavior.

Many technology companies, for example, like Microsoft, have strong cash profits and large cash balances, but pay no dividend. They will have enormous latitude to increase their share prices by introducing a dividend and paying large special dividends out of current cash balances. Other companies that are principally debt-financed will benefit very little initially, but have broad scope to increase value by selling shares to reduce debt.

Shareholders will exert pressure on managers to increase dividend payouts and deleverage their businesses. Managers who own stock or stock options will gladly agree to do so. They will increase payout ratios out of current profits and sell new stock to finance growth. And, they will sell new stock to repay debt. Both will increase stock prices. The upward limit of the resulting rise in stock prices ranges between 50% and 60% for different sectors. This could add 5% or more per year to total returns for several years as companies adjusted to new tax rates.

# Why Dividend and Capital Gains Tax Rates are Important for Growth

The clamor for protectionism in response to trade deficit numbers with China drowns out every other issue. But the key to U.S. growth and trade is not bashing the Chinese currency—it's the tax bills that will emerge from Congress. At stake—tax rates on the capital that determines our productivity and workers' paychecks.

America is not competing for jobs with China. We are competing for capital. Double-taxing dividend and capital gains income drives capital to China where it earns higher after-tax returns. When that happens, American workers are left behind with falling productivity and uncompetitive companies.

Reducing or eliminating dividend and capital gains tax rates keeps capital in the U.S., where it makes workers productive and supports high incomes. Congress must act now to keep rates from increasing in 2010 by extending or eliminating dividend and capital gains taxes.

The 2003 cuts in both dividend and capital gains tax rates hit the stock market and corporate boardrooms like a bunker buster. The Dow Jones Industrial Average almost doubled in the four years after 12/31/02, one week before President Bush announced the dividend and capital gains tax rate cuts.

Dividend and capital gains tax cuts are not trickle-down economics, as claimed by opponents. They work by jolting asset markets, stock prices and capital spending, and by altering business decisions about capital structure, dividend payout and capital deployment.

In December 2002, I prepared a report based on the material in this chapter for a White House working group. It detailed how the dividend tax cut would impact the U.S. stock market and its major sectors through two different channels: 1) recapitalizing the stock market, and 2) restructuring corporate balance sheets.

The restructuring impact of tax cuts on stock prices plays out over several years, but is potentially several times larger than the initial price impact. The 2003 tax cuts were larger for dividend income (from 38.6% to 15%) than for capital gains income (20% to 15%); tax rates on interest income were unchanged. This made the impact on a stock's value greater: the greater its profitability, the greater the percentage of equity—rather than debt—in its capital structure, the greater its payout rate and the greater its duration. (A stock with a greater duration is more sensitive to changes in cost of capital.)

In 2003, U.S. companies were poorly structured to benefit from the changes. Decades of high dividend tax rates and deductible interest payments had encouraged managers to finance companies with debt instead of equity, which reduced profits and increased bankruptcy risk, and to reinvest profits and hoard cash for acquisitions rather than pay out dividends, regardless of the company's prospects. According to the American Shareholders Association, the number of S&P 500 companies paying dividends fell from 469 in 1980 to 351 in 2002. By 2002, the S&P 900 (large and mid-cap) companies were financed with only 27% equity and 73% debt.

Once tax rates were cut in 2003, managers quickly learned they could profit from lower tax rates by restructuring balance sheets (issuing equity to buy back debt, e.g., Nextel), initiating new dividends and cleaning out their cash hoards through one-time special dividends (e.g., Microsoft), and increasing dividend payout ratios. As a result, dividend payments received by shareholders have more than doubled since the tax cuts.

As companies, one by one, made these changes, their equity values increased. But changing capital structure takes time—one reason I believe equities will enjoy strong returns for many years *if* tax rates remain low.

We need permanent tax cuts, not temporary extensions, to fully realize these benefits. Managers do not make decisions about leverage and dividend payouts lightly. They will restructure only if they believe tax rates will remain low. But Congress will only give them temporary rate cuts and temporary extensions in order to comply with the bizarre Congressional budget scoring ritual.

Equities are a long-term investment. Based on our estimates, the duration of the S&P 500 is over 26 years. Each of the first five future years of expected free cash flow contributes only about 2% of the stock market's intrinsic value. That means 96% of the value of the stock market depends on expected after-tax profits *after* 2010, the date when the tax cuts are currently scheduled to expire. We need to make tax cuts permanent so investors will fully reflect them in stock prices.

Congress can extend today's low rates temporarily and keep the recovery strong and net worth growing. Better still, they could make current tax rates permanent, which would encourage managers to speed up restructuring activities, accelerate stock market gains, reduce cost of capital and increase capital spending. Best, they should end double taxation by making both dividend and capital gains rates permanently zero.

America enjoys the highest living standards in the world because American workers enjoy the use of the largest and most advanced stock of tools in the world. But tools are mobile; workers are not. While America continues to double-tax capital income through dividend and capital gains taxes, China, India and other countries are aggressively competing for American capital with increasingly investor-friendly policies.

When the capital leaves, the paycheck goes with it. We can't afford to let that happen.

# 9

# The Neuroscience of Fear

C ognitive science is a relatively new interdisciplinary field that combines neurology, psychology, evolutionary systems biology, mathematics, far-from-equilibrium physics, communications theory and computer modeling to learn how our brains process information about the external environment. I have spent a ton of time over the past fifteen years getting up to speed on the work in this area. It is one of the most exciting research fields today.

I am especially interested in the work on how we acquire, process and respond to fear, and in the research linking fear and conflict among individuals, cultures and nations. My wife Pamela's Ph.D. dissertation is on this topic, so I get an inside look at the literature. Recent work has shown that prolonged states of fear lead to physical changes in the structure of our brains. These changes make us behave in a way that makes it more likely that we will engage in conflict with others.

Eric Kandel (2006)—the man who made the giant sea slug (Aplysia) famous—won the Nobel Prize in Physiology in 2000 for his work on short and long-term memory formation and storage. One of his contributions was to clarify the physical difference between short-term and long-term memory formation. Short-term memory works by temporarily changing the chemistry in the synapses, or gaps, between neurons. In contrast, long-term memory works by triggering the physical growth of new presynaptic terminals. The resulting increase in the number of synaptic connections persists as long as the memory is retained. In other words, a sustained state of fear rewires your brain.

In one experiment, Kandel and his colleagues found that a single Aplysia sensory neuron has approximately 1,300 synaptic terminals, with which it contacts about 25 different target cells. Of the 1,300 presynaptic terminals, only about 40% have active synapses. The remaining terminals are dormant.

If you subject the neuron to a series of unpleasant stimuli, however, an experiment known as long-term sensitization, "the number of synaptic terminals more than doubles from 1,300 to 2,700, and the proportion of active synapses increases from 40% to 60%. In addition, there is an outgrowth from motor neurons to receive some of the new connections" (page 214).

This makes sense, because in nature, an animal that experiences a frightening situation will be more likely to survive a second occurrence if it learns to respond more quickly the next time it encounters a similar situation.

What makes less sense is that the physical changes caused by long-term exposure to fear are, at least partly, permanent. Kandel found that once the increase in synaptic terminals has taken place, removing the fear-generating stimulus leads to a gradual decrease in the number of connections over time, but to a number that is substantially higher than the initial figure. In other words, prolonged exposure to fear leads, at least partially, to a permanently aroused state of hyper-vigilance.

Why does this matter? Because over the last decade, Americans have been subjected to an endless stream of both terrifyingly real and imagined frightening events. We have lived through the dot-com bust, Y2K, the Enron and MCI scandals, Sarbanes-Oxley, 9/11, anthrax, SAARS, mad cow disease, bird flu, Katrina, Afghanistan, Iraq, $120/barrel oil, the subprime mortgage meltdown, airport security alerts and global warming.

This prolonged state of fear has negative long-term health effects. Fear also has long-term effects on investors' ability to make sound judgments about risk and return. Frightened investors have been sitting on their cash, staying out of the stock market for fear of losing their money.

Prolonged exposure to fear also has debilitating effects on societies, as Wexler (2006) shows in his important book *Brain and Culture*. Brain circuits are highly plastic during the early years of a person's life, i.e., they are able to physically adapt to perform well in the environment they experience.

By early adulthood, however, we lose much of this plasticity. If a person experiences a sudden change of environment after losing brain plasticity, he or she experiences profound mental discomfort, or cognitive dissonance, due to the inconsistencies between internal mental structures and the external environment. We respond by building virtual walled communities. We unconsciously engage in selective perception. We seek information that confirms our internal structures and avoid information that conflicts with our beliefs. We aggregate into affiliative networks with other like-minded people by seeking out people, reading material, news and entertainment that reinforce our sense of order. We ignore, discredit or forget offending information.

Information providers, such as television networks, radio networks, newspapers, magazines and blogs amplify this behavior by providing selective information streams that deliver cognitive consonance to their viewers, listeners or readers. They do not necessarily do it out of philosophical or political bias; they do it because it is good business.

This stream of filtered information reinforces the isolation of in-group members from the outside world. Government leaders exploit and amplify people's fears to gain and hold power. In today's world of faster information flows and more rapid change, however, the walls cannot hold. Isolated cultures are ripe for conflict at the slightest provocation from outside groups. This is a description of the dynamic system that leads to wars.

Later in this chapter, I will write about an especially important application of these ideas—relations between the U.S. and China over the coming decades. First, though, I want to make the case that, at least for investors, fear is for tourists.

## Ricardo's Rule

David Ricardo (1817) was a British economist in the early nineteenth-century who first wrote about the principle of comparative advantage. The principle argues that trade between two countries raises GDP in both countries by allowing people to specialize in what they do relatively best. Based upon recent news reports, nobody in Congress has read Ricardo.

Ricardo was also a great investor. He had one simple rule: things are never as bad or as good as people think they are. From time to time, people allow their emotions to carry away their reason. They either get delirious and push prices to unsustainably high levels or they panic and force prices to collapse. Either way worked for Ricardo—he always bet against the emotions of crowds. He was usually right. He made enough money to buy a borough in Ireland—a place he never visited—which gave him a long black robe and a seat in the House of Lords. Not bad for a commodity trader. Ricardo's advice is as good today as it was then.

## Why We Panic

The interesting question is not *if* people panic—of course we do—it is *why* we panic.

Ricardo knew something that we should remember. Spiking or collapsing stock prices and commodity prices rarely reflect important or fundamental events for economies or companies. They reflect something happening in investors' brains.

This is especially true of long trends during which the same change has been repeated over and over again. These periods give us an inflated sense of order and security, and cause us to overestimate our investment acumen and our degree of control over our lives. The Greeks called it *hubris*—the illusion that one can speak directly with the Gods. Investors call it momentum. It was the source of both the dot-com bubble and the subprime mortgage crisis.

No one has repealed the second law of thermodynamics, however, which guarantees that entropy—the tendency towards disorder, not order—rules. Beware hubris. At the point you begin to believe you are especially good at whatever you do, you should go lie down until the feeling goes away.

## Why We Crave Order

There are physical and psychological reasons why we crave order. Physicists refer to people, animals and all living matter as dissipative systems, highly ordered temporary structures that must continually process energy or die. Without a continual bath of oxygen, water, food, heat, and other sources of energy, we quickly decay. We are dependent upon physical order every minute of every day. We are terrified by chaos and by disorder.

History is filled with examples of people who love individual freedom and liberty, but who quickly sacrifice their freedoms when their sense of order has been threatened. Almost all our literature (*Othello*) and much of our music (Beethoven's *Fifth Symphony*) are designed to reinforce our sense of order by constructing tales in which order, threatened by chaos, is ultimately restored through the valiant efforts of man or God. The struggle between order (Heaven) and chaos (Hell) is the core of western philosophy and western religions.

## The Witch Hunt

People do terrible things when their sense of order has been threatened. Savonarola's rise and fall in Florence at the time of the plague, the Inquisition, the Salem witch trials, the reign of terror in post-revolution France, the expulsion of Jews from Isabella's Spain, the persecution of Jews in Depression Germany, the imprisonment of American citizens of Japanese descent in California during World War II, the McCarthy hearings and recent human rights abuses in post-9/11 America are all examples.

After all, when something goes wrong, we have to blame somebody. Otherwise we would have to come to terms with the fact that the world is a frightening and disorderly place—everywhere, every day. Once we pick someone to blame, we "*other*" that person, in psychological terms, denying his or her right to be a member of our tribe. The worst crimes against people in history have been committed against *othered* groups. The greater the perceived difference between our own group and others, the more likely we are to negatively stereotype them, assume they are up to no good, and view them as a threat.

For most Americans today, the Arab world fits our *othering* criteria nicely. They live a long way away. Their complexions are (just a little bit) darker than (some of) ours. They speak a language we don't understand that doesn't even use our alphabet—how dare they! They have a history and a religion most Americans know almost nothing about. And they have all that darned oil. Arabs are an easy target for frightened Americans today.

China is another great *othering* opportunity for Americans. And for the same reasons. They live even farther away on the other side of the earth. They look different than (some of) us. They speak a language with tones that most Americans can't even hear. And they use a writing system that is based on pictograms and sounds and doesn't resemble a western alphabet at all! The Communist party runs their government. They were our enemies during the Cold War. Very few Americans have ever visited China. And it is virtually impossible to get a positive story about China through the American media.

Often, we blame the "priests"—all those in positions of leadership—for letting us down. News reports are filled with scandals about Catholic priests, televangelists, and their secular cousins, the auditors, ratings agencies, analysts and CEOs. Anyone who had the temerity to rise to a leadership position is at risk. The stories about Enron, Arthur Andersen, Global Crossing, TYCO, Xerox, WorldCom, Martha Stewart, mortgage brokers and investment bankers reveal more about our carnivorous appetites and need to find a sacrificial lamb to restore order than about their behavior. In election years and hard economic times, we place blame outside our tribe for lost jobs and slowing economic prospects by espousing protectionist policies. In the short-term, this strategy is a sure vote getter. In the long term, rewiring people's brains to be fearful and antagonistic toward others is a very dangerous game to play.[1]

---

[1] Interestingly, recent work in evolutionary biology suggests that aggression between two groups, or systems, may be a result of the system architecture rather than a result of conscious decisions by individual agents within the systems. As mentioned previously, Deborah Gordon (2000) has shown that foraging ants from young ant colonies are more likely to attack, and foraging ants from mature colonies more likely to avoid conflict, when they experience encounters while hunting for food. This is true in spite of the fact that foragers only live for one year while the queen and therefore the colony may live from 12-15 years, and there is no communication from the queen to the foragers. Apparently systems can possess wisdom not appreciated by their members.

## China on the Horizon

China's rapid economic growth and huge population make her the only likely challenger to the global economic, political and military dominance that the U.S. has enjoyed for many years. Technology has created a global marketplace that continues to change faster than humans can adjust. U.S. workers and businesses find themselves having to compete with China for jobs, factories, investment capital and natural resources like oil, gas, copper and lead. The old rules have changed. Capital can travel the world; the worker has to compete with other guys just like him across the globe, not just across town. And 1.3 billion of those guys are in China. In 2007, China was directly responsible for more than one-third of global economic growth. China's role will be increasingly important to the world and the U.S. for years to come; and our policy decisions directly impact our relationship with China, for better or worse.

China has committed to fully opening capital markets as part of the WTO process. This will have important impacts on both the Chinese and American economies. We can best understand the impact of opening capital markets on the economies of China and the U.S. by using the laws of thermodynamic systems from Chapter 6.

China and the U.S. have been effectively closed economic systems for most of the past six decades. A closed system is one in which temperature, pressure and other state variables are everywhere driven to uniformity. In economics, we refer to closed systems as "markets." A market is defined as the area in which price tends toward uniformity. This is known as "the law of one price." In closed economic systems, prices, wages, incomes, the price of capital and the return on capital are determined by local supply and demand conditions, by population, and by existing stocks of both human and non-human capital.

Dramatic changes in China during the past 30 years have brought these formerly closed economic systems into close communication. This has been caused by changes in laws and regulations, China's WTO membership and the opening of Chinese capital markets.

When formerly closed economic systems are brought into contact to form one large closed system, the speed at which prices and wages are driven together depends on the 'bandwidth' of the channel connecting the systems. Traditionally, these adjustments have occurred as a result of trade in goods, where bandwidth is limited by shipping capacity. Like the washtubs with a small hole in the wall from Chapter 6, this makes the resulting adjustments slow.

More recently, changes in communications technology, in the form of information technology (IT) and fiber-optic communications, have broadened and deepened these channels, dramatically increasing channel bandwidth. The small hole in the side of the washtub is now a gash, releasing torrents, not dribbles. This has greatly accelerated convergence of prices, wages and returns on capital *across* markets, not within them. For the first time, the adjustments are primarily driven by changes in the service sectors, i.e. by changes in wage rates.

Open capital markets are very important for China. In order to continue to grow at high rates and to develop its energy resources, China must import growing amounts of foreign direct investment and technology. Fully open capital markets will reduce risks to foreign investors and make the investor's decision about where to locate capital more responsive to return differentials. This will accelerate the flow of foreign direct investment (FDI) to China from the United States, Europe and Japan, and will allow China's economy to sustain high growth for decades to come.

As a result, two formerly closed systems—the U.S. and China—will become one system. Flows of capital and labor services will drive relative prices, wages, incomes and returns together.

Economic convergence raises several issues:

1. What will the new set of relative prices and wages look like?

2. Will the transition be smooth? Or marred by disruptive stops and starts?

3. How will the changes impact domestic politics and policies in both countries?

The new relative prices will tend toward the mass-weighted average of current relative prices in both countries. We know this has to happen because of the second law of thermodynamics. Although prices and wages will change substantially in both countries, changes will be larger and more disruptive in China because the Chinese economy is much smaller than the U.S. economy. This does not mean there won't be pain felt by U.S. workers in places like Detroit and Indiana. U.S. manufacturing firms will not be able to sustain current payrolls and benefits levels and still be competitive in the global economy, so workers unable to transition to other jobs will be left behind.

Given the speed of technological innovation and advancement, the adjustment is unlikely to be smooth. As I discussed earlier, chaotic, unpredictable change frightens people and leads to political pressures on governments for 'protection' to do the impossible—stop change. These political pressures in both countries can give rise to destructive short-term policy reactions—such as tariffs, quotas, or pressure to change exchange rates—that can have permanent effects, making adjustments worse, not better.

The goal of policymakers should be to make the adjustment as stable and orderly as possible, not to use fear as an opportunity to drive psychological wedges between groups of people within and outside of the country. Rapid change calls for increased mutual understanding of history, culture and language to counteract the natural knee-jerk tendency to blame the other guy.

## Forget the Renminbi, Revalue the Latte

One of the common refrains out of Washington has been trying to get China to revalue their currency to "level the playing field." This is a dumb idea for a lot of reasons, including the risk of massive social unrest in China and making all Americans pay more for goods to artificially preserve uncompetitive manufacturing sectors in the U.S., not to mention the bad manners of bullying other people into changing their policies—which, by the way, only works while you're still the only big guy.

On a recent trip to China to better understand the implications of U.S. pressure on Beijing to revalue the Renminbi (RMB), I uncovered a story you won't see any place else. In a terrific piece of investigative journalism, I have discovered that Starbucks has revalued the latte in China. It's a little difficult to read the type in the "stealth photo" I took with my little spy camera at a Beijing Starbucks—I spend a lot of time there—but if you look closely you will see that the three cup sizes in the photo are not the Venti, Grande, and Tall that we are familiar with in the U.S.; but Grande, Tall, and Short. Someone has kidnapped the Venti.

The prices of the three sizes, translated into U.S. dollars, were about equal to what we would pay in the U.S., which means the "per ounce" prices in China are actually higher, not lower, as many Americans believe. Using one ounce of cappuccino—defined by Wikipedia as 1/3 espresso, 1/3 steamed milk, and 1/3 foam—as the unit of account, I have determined that, measured in U.S. dollars, one unit of cappuccino is 50% more expensive in Beijing (the tall/short volume ratio being 12/8=1.5) than it is in the United States.

This discovery has major implications for global currency markets. Instead of revaluing the RMB by 25% as the U.S. government wants, my research indicates that China should actually devalue the RMB by 50% to restore Cappuccino Purchasing Power Parity (CPPP) and correct global imbalances. I am trying to get this information to Treasury Secretary Paulson before his meetings in Beijing to avoid a potentially disastrous policy mistake that could have global repercussions.

## Win in China

In a sign of just how capitalist Communist China has become, the hottest television sensation on the mainland is a game show—for entrepreneurs.

Much like *The Apprentice*—with a dash of *American Idol* mixed in—*Win in China* pits aspiring moguls against each other. The top prize: 10 million Renminbi ($1.4 million) in venture capital to finance their business plan, and a fifth of the equity in the new company. To win, contestants have to convince the judges—successful venture capitalists, CEOs, the audience and me, the only western judge—that their business plan has the right stuff.

The force behind the show is Wang Lifen (Anna), a long-time executive producer of *Dialogue*, CCTV-2's popular interview show. While on sabbatical in America, Anna witnessed the explosive growth of shows like *Survivor* and *American Idol*—but she wanted to build a show based on Chinese values: innovation and entrepreneurship.

"Every young Chinese person wants to realize their dreams," Anna told me recently in Beijing. "The best way to realize dreams is start-ups."

You might think China isn't ready for an entrepreneurial revolution. Despite decades of economic reform, state-owned enterprises still play a prominent role in the economy. And traditionally, businessmen are looked down upon and depicted as corrupt in China, while government leaders, scholars and workers are highly respected.

But the success of *Win in China* has shattered such stereotypes. The program shows the hard work it takes to build a business, especially in the IT sector. "Entrepreneurs are the heroes of our peaceful times," Anna explains. "They make employment and pay taxes. Our country can only be rich if we have a lot of entrepreneurs."

Twelve finalists compete in a series of events focused on accomplishing business tasks. In one episode, they hit the streets in teams to sell insurance to real people. In another, they designed and executed an operation to distribute free dairy products to schools in poor villages. In another, they raised funds for a charity. In the finale, the audience selected the winner using SMS messages.

The prize? Donald Trump, eat your heart out. It is not a job as somebody's personal assistant. The winner not only gets 10 million RMB in venture capital financing; he'll own 20% of the equity in the new company. Half of the remaining equity goes to the venture capital firms that fund the deal, and the rest to text-messaging viewers and to CCTV itself.

But to be successful, real-world entrepreneurs need access to all types of capital—tools, education, training and technology. As I wrote in the last chapter, countries are not competing for jobs today; they are competing for capital. The various forms of capital—modern tools, education, training, technology and working capital—are what make workers productive.

Governments who ignore these changes in capital mobility do so at the peril of their workers' paychecks. Some governments get it; some don't. It will come as a surprise to most Americans that China gets it, and is changing policies to educate and train entrepreneurs and attract foreign capital.

## America's Autoimmune Disorder

As you know, I believe that changes in communications technology are among the most important drivers in the world today. The rapid change in information access and flows is a big factor in psychological and social discomfort. Access to information from around the world is also a powerful motivator for change.

People from Colombia to Kenya and Buffalo to Bangalore can now watch each other wake up every day. People in poor countries watch our TV shows. They have determined that Americans are very rich, and it is probably not because Americans are smarter, work harder, or are better looking than they are—it is our access to capital. They have learned that they are poor and they don't like it. We have to come to terms with these broadening lines of communication, and figure out how to use them to grow and learn together.

Viewers in rich countries can now see just how poor their neighbors are every day. Some choose to ignore it. Some are trying to do things to help poor people improve their lives. Some react by turning the people in poor countries into demagogues, making them responsible for all our problems. Most of all, people become frightened they will lose their wealth and living standards. That's why this is such a politically contentious time, both in the U.S. and around the world.

I don't have time to be scared—there is too much to do. I don't have much patience for people who use their energy being scared. And

I have total contempt for those who frighten people for political or eco-nomic gain. Fortunately, throughout history, frightened people usually adapt and go back to their normal activities. And when they do, inves-tors will pump the $2 trillion in cash they are sitting on back into the stock market, and managers will plow their cash hoards back into capital spending. I want to be there when the prices go up.

It's a big mistake to crawl into your bunker every time a news story from Iran, Venezuela, China and other places hits the wires.

Over the past 40 years, I have traveled 15 million miles, wandered around South America, Eastern Europe, Northern Africa and Asia, and I have made dozens of trips to the Middle East. I have good friends in all those places. I have been searched by 16-year-old soldiers with machine guns; I have been detained by officials with stars on their shoulders but no brains in their heads. I have been in air raids and food riots. I have even been stopped by tanks. I am still here. My conclusions:

1. The world has never been safe, and it never will be. Deal with it.

2. There are 300 million of us here in the United States; who-ever is mad at us can't get us all.

3. The biggest risk is not the risk of dying; it is the risk of not living.

It is not possible to spend enough money to protect people from other people who may want to hurt them. The result would be man-on-man defense, just like in basketball. When I was 18 years old, I lived for a time in West Berlin. I used to go for walks every evening along the Berlin Wall—actually, a fence and a mine field—and wave at the East German guards in the machine gun towers every fifty meters or so. The guards on the other side of the fence were assigned to duty in pairs so they could keep an eye on each other. They never waved back. They were not having fun.

We should not pretend that we can deliver total security. People should take more responsibility themselves for being alert to danger and get on with their lives.

The real price of delivering excessive imaginary protection is not the money we pay the TSA employees at the airports, it is our loss of identity, which is a form of autoimmune disorder.

Biological immune systems do not work by having a list of bad guys to look for. They work by being able to recognize "me." When a healthy immune system encounters a cell, it is able to determine whether the cell is "self," in which case it allows it to pass, or is "other" in which case it attacks, kills or repels the invader.

Autoimmune disorders, such as AIDS, are situations in which the immune system loses the ability to identify itself and makes mistakes with both kinds of cells, killing itself as a result. In other words, autoimmune disorders are the loss of your own identity.

The most damaging long-term effect of terrorism in the U.S. is that we have become so focused on obtaining order that we are losing our identity.

In the case of the U.S., our identity is to take risks, try things, build things and welcome strangers. Fear has driven us into our bunkers, behind our TSA guards, and into racism.

The good news is that we can fix this problem ourselves by remembering who we are.

## The Search for Bird Flu

Pandemics are among the things Americans have been repeatedly told they should worry about. About the time things really started going to hell in Iraq, government officials began waving books about pandemics on TV and telling us that Bird Flu would be the next plague. A number of TV viewers have sent emails accusing me of not taking Bird Flu seriously. I assure you that this is not true. In fact during a recent trip to China I made a special trip to Liaoning province—the epicenter of recent outbreaks—to trace the bird flu to its source. As you will see

from my indisputable photographic proof, my search was not in vain.

My search began at the St. Regis hotel in Beijing, where I discovered this suspicious looking waterfowl lurking near my bathtub. Alas, after making a careful examination of the little fellow while bathing, I determined it was free of the deadly H5N1 virus.

Acting on a hunch, we took a taxi to the Ju De Roast Duck Restaurant, the oldest and most famous in Beijing.

My hopes were dashed when my good friend Kim informed me that all we would find at Ju De would be the most delicious crispy roast duck in the world—bird flu was not on the menu that day. Our hunger for the truth unsated, we consoled ourselves with a plate of roast duck,

pancakes and plum sauce, washed down (strictly for antiseptic purposes) with a tall, cold mug of Tsingtao beer. Undaunted, I continued my search.

Finding no virus in Beijing, I flew north to Shenyang in the heart of the Chinese poultry region to do a series of lectures to help our State Department explain the impact of open capital markets on Chinese companies and investors. There, I hit pay dirt. Actually, pay bird.

With the help of my State Department hosts, I determined that this giant duck in front of the best duck restaurant in Shenyang started this whole pandemic thing. I had no choice. For the good of the world, I decided to eat him before he could strike again. He was delicious.

## The 1918 *Influenza A* Virus

I want to be serious about the flu virus for a moment. The lead article in the November 24, 2005 issue of *The New England Journal of Medicine* is a must-read for anyone who wants to make sense out of the hand-wringing in the media about the risk of the bird flu virus mutating into something that can spread from human to human.

The article was written by Dr. Robert Belshe, Professor in the Division of Infectious Diseases and Immunology at St. Louis University. It is titled "The Origins of Pandemic Influenza—Lessons from the 1918 Virus." In the article, Dr. Belshe discusses the implications of the spectacular recent completion of the genetic sequencing of the 1918 *influenza A* virus by Taubenberger et. al, reported in an article in the October 6, 2005 issue of *Nature*, and in a subsequent article in *Science* in which Tumpey et. al. used Taubenberger's sequence to recreate the complete 1918 virus.

The Taubenberger paper provides strong evidence that the 1918 (Spanish flu) virus was derived solely from a virus that originally infected birds, in contrast to its descendents, the 1957 (Asian flu) and 1968 (Hong Kong flu) viruses that arose when human and bird flu viruses infected the same person at the same time, allowing the genes to mix—a process known as reassortment. "Today, the descendents of this virus continue to cause the majority of influenza infections in humans."

I urge you to read the Belshe article, which contains an eye-opening schematic of the specific mechanisms by which the 1918 Spanish flu was transformed into the 1957 Asian flu, then the 1968 Hong Kong flu, as well as the genetic events which might be required in order to make the current H5N1 avian flu virus capable of adapting to humans.

My take-aways from the articles:

1. The bird flu is not new. Virtually all human flu cases since 1918 have been descendents of the 1918 flu virus, which was contracted from birds.

2. The good news: the genetic events that must take place to make the current bird flu capable of adapting to replicate among humans are extremely complex, therefore, extremely unlikely. More likely is a new pathogen that we are not even thinking about today.

3. The bad news: pandemics happen. Plagues and pandemics have been a recurring story since the beginning of recorded history. It is highly improbable that we have seen the last one. Deal with it.

4. The other good news: as ethologists write about, pathogens (the virus) and hosts (you and me) together form a system of mutual survival and interdependence. Scientists refer to dynamic equilibrium in these systems as ESS, Evolutionary Stable Systems, in which hosts and pathogens are killing each other off at just the right rates to sustain current population parameters. In such systems, the adaptation of each makes the other stronger. It is nature's form of competition.

One of the most fascinating studies I have read was conducted by a group of biologists who compared the random mutations of rat mitochondria (the little fuel processing organelles in each of our cells that have their own, much simpler DNA) during episodes of widespread plague and during normal periods. They found that mitochondrial DNA mutations occurred three times faster in the presence of virulent pathogens (during plagues) than during normal times.

I think this is precisely the system property that makes the U.S. economy more robust and adaptable than most other major economies. As American business owners and managers can tell you, in the U.S., competitors try to kill your business every day, forcing adaptation, cost cutting, rationalizing, restructuring, soul-searching and, ultimately, growth. Without the relentless attacks of pathogens (your competitors), none of this would happen.

My final, final, take-away from the articles is that we should give the viruses all the respect they deserve and devote sufficient resources to combat them over time. But we should not allow the presence of a virus to debilitate us with fear. Bird flu should be fought in the laboratories, not in press conferences.

There is one further cost of the current pandemic fear. We are neglecting the real problem. The probability that bird flu will become a human pandemic is very low. But the probability that the bird flu will cause massive hardships and hunger among the low-income farmers in China, Vietnam and elsewhere in Asia is very real. In China, it is accepted practice to kill all poultry within 3 kilometers of a reported case of avian flu. Millions of poor farmers whose flocks are being destroyed are losing their only means of making a living, an event with potentially massive political and economic implications for everyone.

## From Bird Flu to Enron

During the Enron investigation, I wrote an article for my friends at the *American Spectator* about the lessons we could take away from the experience. Here are a few of them.

Don't worry. I'm not actually going to write about Enron. The really interesting thing isn't what Enron did anyway; it's what the story reveals about us, the way we process information, and the way we make investment decisions.

Why did we discover it when we did? Why didn't we know what was going on? Why were we so outraged? Why did we watch the C-SPAN witch trials when we knew the inquisitors were on the payroll too? How did it affect risk taking? How did it affect the stock market?

We need to know how you and I stepped on the biggest banana peel in history, proving for all time that God does have a sense of humor.

Unlike economists, physicists are used to looking in the mirror. To them the observer is an integral part of the system being observed— the essence of Niels Bohr's Copenhagen Interpretation of quantum mechanics. According to Bohr, the answer to the famous question about a tree falling in the forest is simple: if nobody is there to see it, the tree doesn't even exist!

So it is for economics and financial markets too. In economics, the observer, i.e., the investor, determines asset prices by setting both the risk-adjusted cost of capital and the expectations for future cash flows. These prices then feed back through credit markets, collateral values, and analyst and rating agency announcements to further influence asset prices. When all this goes wrong, as it did with Enron, apparent value can evaporate overnight.

Here are some questions that highlight our own role in the disaster.

## Why Did Enron Appear in the Headlines When It Did?

Our first question concerns timing. Not the timing of the Enron events—they had been going on for years. Why did we notice them when we did?

Here's the principal reason: the incredible 1981-2001 stock market rise, during which you could make money in the stock market with Valley Girl ("What-ever") stock selection, was over. For twenty years, interest rates had gone down and stock prices had gone up. During that extraordinary period, the market did not reward caution. Statisticians call such an improbably long run of luck—flipping a coin and getting twenty heads in a row—a *race*. Wall Street calls it a bull market. Either way, it encourages people to place big uninformed bets and keep their winnings in the game.

Cognitive science researchers such as William Calvin, author of *The Cerebral Code*, argue that our brains process information by extracting patterns, or metaphors, from the observed world and projecting them into the future. Twenty heads in a row is a pattern few stock market investors were willing to bet against. They were an accident waiting to happen.

The tech bubble bust, credit crunch and recession sobered people up. The California energy crunch gave them a scare. The September 11th attacks sealed the deal. It is no coincidence that Enron vaporized in the weeks just after 9/11—investors' appetites for risk collapsed with the World Trade Center.

## Why Were We Surprised?

Apparently Abe Lincoln was wrong—you can fool all the people for a long time. At least you can in the public markets.

Public market investors are like mushrooms; they live mostly in the dark. Ironically, the insider trading rules that are designed to protect outside investors have built barriers of silence around public companies. Public company managers—whether out of disdain for public shareholders or fear of running afoul of the SEC's complex rules regarding dissemination of material information—keep their cards close to their vests. They hire investor relations staff to keep investors and analysts at arms length, and conduct discussions with them only in tightly controlled venues. They produce consolidated, i.e., unintelligible, financial statements.

As a further irony, the bigger the company, the harder it is for an investor to find out what is really going on.

Finally, Wall Street analysts are just too young. More than three quarters of analysts lost their jobs during the bear market from 1968 to 1981. Everyone working on Wall Street today still has all their hair. They have not yet lived through a bear market. Not good.

Contrast this with companies owned by entrepreneurs and private equity investors, who have access to every document and person in a company, who can ask any employee any question at any time, who take part in planning the company's future, and who can intervene and make changes when necessary. The owner of a corner drug store knows more about what's going on inside his business than public investors or stock market analysts will ever know about public companies like Enron.

There are people who know what's going on in public companies, of course. Unfortunately, they are either the hired managers with salaries and one-way stock options with no money in the game, or investment bankers, lawyers and other hired guns working for fees. Until we find a way to make them put their own money at risk in the company's stock, we shouldn't be surprised at the shabby way shareholders get treated.

## Why Are We Angry?

As I keep writing, man is an order-seeking creature. Unfortunately, the world is a disorderly place and getting more so, guaranteed by the monotonically increasing entropy dictated by the second law of thermodynamics. We bridge this uncomfortable gap, the cognitive dissonance I mentioned above, by wrapping ourselves in a cocoon of illusion that the world—our world, at least—is safe.

This sense of order was shattered when we watched hi-jacked airliners crash into the World Trade Center. It was further eroded when we learned we could not trust public-company financial statements or the people who audit their books. We will do almost anything to restore our illusion of order so that we can go about our business in comfort again. Throughout history, the standard way to accomplish this is to burn someone at the stake. Anyone will do.

## Why Do We Love to Watch Witch Trials?

No, this is not Salem, fifteenth century Spain or the McCarthy era. Yes, we are still having witch trials. In America, we use politicians to conduct our exorcisms. We hold them on C-SPAN so everyone can watch.

History gives us many examples of frightened people behaving badly. It forms the basis for Shakespeare's *Othello*, for Voltaire's *Candide*, for Dickens's *A Tale of Two Cities*, for Charles MacKay's *Popular Delusions* and the *Madness of Crowds*, and for Freud's treatise on mob psychology in Hitler's Germany. It gave us the Inquisition, the Ku Klux Klan and Joe McCarthy.

With Enron, the mob was out for blood, looking for bad guys under every balance sheet. After Enron and Arthur Andersen, the spotlight shifted to Tyco, Vivendi, Global Crossing and many others. The mob is never satisfied until its illusion of order has been restored. Let's hope that happens quickly.

It is critical that we take the steps to restore the credibility of our managers, our companies and our financial statements in the eyes of investors around the world. It is even more critical that we do so with fairness, decency and respect for our institutions.

## How Does Fear Affect The Stock Market?

Stock market investors build a liar's premium into the cost of capital, which they use to discount public companies' expected future cash flows. As a result, the stock market followed the Enron story down like synchronized pair skaters. The Enron saga also made stock prices extremely volatile, and made the shares of even established companies with huge market capitalizations react violently to every bit of new information.

This was and is a harsh environment for investors who don't do their own homework, and belies a serious structural problem in the market. In recent years, investors have developed an unhealthy and excessive reliance on the work of rating agencies and sell-side securities analysts when making valuation judgments. Investors who are willing to take positions based upon independent judgments about intrinsic value play an important stabilizing market-maker role. As their numbers dwindle, whether due to indexing or increased reliance on a small group of third-party advisors, stock prices become more volatile. Essentially, the market is deprived of the normalizing benefits of the Central Limit Theorem, which says, roughly, that the average behavior of a large number of independent events becomes more predictable as the number of events increases.

In a similar way, lenders, vendors and stock market investors have all developed an unhealthy dependence on rating agencies. Automatic triggers have increasingly been built into contracts of all sorts, which change input prices, interest rates, credit availability and other important business parameters based upon changes in the credit ratings of a company's outstanding securities. These triggers depend on the decisions of just a few people at only three rating agencies, rather than the average behavior of a large number of investors. The result is the increasingly chaotic price movements we have seen—such as Enron's own cliff dive.

Mathematicians know that systems with both delayed feedback mechanisms (reporting delays and reliance on outsiders for information) and nonlinearities (triggers) are unstable. They react to slight disturbances with chaotic swings. Both phenomena are clearly present in the markets today.

Investors who are willing to look in the mirror with the courage to understand our own weaknesses are better equipped to take advantage of times like these. For those who do their own homework, make their own valuation judgments and make their own risk assessments, this is a great time to place your bets.

## Taking Risk

Gun-shy after everything from Enron to bird flu to the subprime mortgage crisis, everyone is backing away from risk. This is as true of the professionals, the banks and insurance companies—who take risk for a living—as it is for the man on the street. Banks have decided that looking after their wealthy clients' money is better business than taking credit risk. Insurance companies are backing away from liability coverage. Stock market investors have voted with their feet, moving into bonds and hedge funds, with the hope of less volatile—but still positive—returns. Too many Americans want politicians to (pretend to) keep them safe from terrorists, job loss, globalization, overeating, retirement and natural disasters.

Our willingness to take risks has always been one of the great strengths of the American people and the American economy. Risk aversion undermines capital investment, innovation, new business formation and growth. Fear has never been the defining characteristic of Americans. I have great hopes that with a little encouragement, Americans will reclaim our identities and rise to the challenge by encouraging entrepreneurship, rewarding (not penalizing) success, and using technology to educate ourselves and our children, so that the U.S. can compete in the 21st century—not just whine about the good old days.

# 10

## Conclusion

### Why I Go To China

About the time we were wrapping up the investment of our second private equity fund, my dad learned that he had a particularly virulent form of lung cancer. I was able to spend a great deal of time with him in the remaining two years of his life. My time with him convinced me that I should focus my energies on doing the things that I love: learning new things, teaching them to people and doing things that can make a difference in the lives of others.

It was clear to me that the epicenter of the global earthquake that was changing the world is in China, so that was where I should go to learn. It was also clear that I could add a lot of value there, both by helping people in China and the U.S. get to know each other, and by developing projects to help young children go to school.

I called the person who was both the smartest person I knew and the one who knew the most about China, my friend Bob Mundell, and asked him if there was something I could do to help his new venture in Beijing, the Mundell International University of Entrepreneurship. He said "come on over."

*With Bob Mundell in 2007*

To state the obvious, Bob is an extraordinary man. His work in the 1960s revolutionized international monetary theory. He invented supply-side economics in the 1970s. He was the driving force behind the adoption of the Euro. And he won the Nobel Prize in economics in 1999. Bob is certainly the greatest economic thinker alive today, my choice for the most influential economist of the 20th century and very possibly of all time.

Since then I have visited China frequently—eleven times in 2007 alone. I have become the Chief Advisor to the Governor of Haidian, China's Silicon Valley. I am an honorary Professor and teach classes at the Graduate University of the Chinese Academy of Sciences, a remarkable institution with 30,000 Ph.D. students in mathematics and the physical sciences. I have worked with Chinese leaders in government and industry. I have made countless TV shows and magazine interviews. Most fun for me, though, is working with the kids, large and small. I have given lectures at universities all over China. And I have a small venture that helps children.

About once every day, someone asks me why I am willing to spend 14 hours on an airplane to get to China every month. I show them this photo.

Not long ago, I visited Changsha, a small city (by Chinese standards) of only 6 million people in Hunan province. I was there to give a lecture and visit with faculty members at Hunan University. I had a wonderful time with the faculty and students there.

During the afternoon, I had a break between classes and decided to take a walk through a local residential neighborhood. While I was walking, these two little girls—maybe 7 years old—came up to me and said "Hello!" in perfect English. I was the only Westerner on the street.

Between their English and my Chinese, we decided to have our picture taken together.

The enthusiasm of young students in China is infectious. They believe in the American Dream, that they can achieve anything through hard work. They are natural friends for Americans. We just have to make the effort to get to know them.

## Meet Tara

Tara lives in my back yard in Maui. I sit with her every morning while I drink my first double espresso of the day. Tara is the goddess of compassion who was born of the petals of a lotus blossom that grew out of the lake of tears that the Buddha shed when he saw the troubles of mankind. She holds her hands in front of her heart in a position (*mudra*) known as *dharmachakra*, which indicates teaching. Her thumb and middle finger touch, which indicates com-

*Tara, Goddess of Compassion*

passion for the suffering of others. To Hindu and Buddhist followers, she is an antidote to ignorance and inhumanity.

I use my morning coffee with Tara to remind myself to be thankful for the incredible bounty I enjoy, to make sure I remember that most of the 6.5 billion people on the planet live in extreme poverty and fear, and to ask whether I am doing the things I want to do to help others. A read of the headlines on any given day indicates that Tara and I still have a lot of work to do.

I recently saw the results of a survey published by the *Hindu*, an Indian newspaper, and the CNN-IBN television network. Among the results: 35% of India's 1.1 billion people went hungry at least once last year and 8% said someone in their family went hungry often.

There was good news too. More than half said their families are eating better than they were 10 years ago. More than half said their consumption of milk, beans and cereals had gone up, and 60% said they eat meat when they can get it.

We hear a lot about the booming Indian economy, growing 8% per year, and we hear about Indian call centers taking American jobs. But we never hear that one-third of India's population—370 million people— lives on less than a dollar a day.

Here are a few background facts to put this in perspective. GDP per capita for the U.S. in 2003 was $37,562 per year, or $102.91 per day, compared with $2,520 per year in India, where 34.7% earned less than $1/day and 79.9% earned less than $2/day. By comparison, China's per capita income in 2003 was $1,087 per year, where 16.6% earned less than $1/day and 46.7% less than $2/day.

More per capita income figures for 2003: World, $8,229; Developing countries, $4,359; Japan, $27,967, Israel, $20,033; Lebanon, $5,074; Saudi Arabia, $13,226; Mexico, $9168; Iran, $6,995; Haiti, $1,742; and Nigeria, $1,050. The life expectancy of a child born in America is 77.4 years; Italy, 80; Japan, 82. In Nigeria it is 43.4; in Haiti, 51.6.

We live in a wonderful, safe and free country. We can afford humanity and compassion towards people inside and outside our country who are not so blessed.

## Fred's Kids

I have two wonderful friends and team members in China. Li Hong (Sunny) worked as a producer for China's top television show and knows every media person, every government official and every business leader in China. She is my Ph.D. student at the Chinese Acad-

*With Sunny and Fred*

emy of Sciences and she works harder than anyone I have ever known. Ko Ysing (Fred) is a serial entrepreneur who teaches business courses at China Agricultural University (CAU). This story is about Fred.

Fred and I both love kids. A few years ago, Fred and I were talking about what we could do for kids and he had a great idea. The President of CAU, Dr. Chen Zhangliang, was a famous genetic biologist, a senior member of the National People's Congress and a passionate mountain climber who had developed a love for Tibetan people. Every summer, Dr. Chen took a group of university students to Tibet to teach the children and to train a group of surgeons in repairing the congenital eye problems of the kids there. (Many Tibetan children need lens replace-

*Me with eight of the seventeen CAU students that volunteered for the month-long trip to Tibet*

ments.) Why didn't we ask Dr. Chen and the CAU students to find a project we could do in Tibet?

It didn't take long for us to recruit a group of seventeen CAU students for our project. Their leader was Ethan, a charismatic senior who wants to be an

entrepreneur. Ethan got help from the Education Ministry to locate a school in Lhasa, Tibet that needed help. He called the headmaster and made arrangements for a summer trip.

Fred and I put together the resources—including more than 5,000 books—to build a new library and provide scholarships to pay the students' school fees in a special school for orphans and disabled children. Ethan's team did all the heavy lifting. The students trained for six months before they made the trip so that they would be fit enough for Lhasa's extreme altitude—Lhasa is the highest capital city in the world, with an altitude of 3,600 meters, or 11,975 feet.

Before the students left on the trip, I met with them in Beijing to talk about the work we would do. The photo on the previous page is a picture I took with "Tara's Warriors" that day. Ethan is the fellow standing behind me wearing the black Rutledge Capital shirt. I asked the students if their parents were worried about them going on such a long trip. The boy on the left holding the gift bag—his English name is "Coffee"—said, "No, they are very proud of us." I asked why they would use up their whole summer to do this. Maggie, the girl in the white dress said, "We just want the children to know that someone loves them."

A lot of people in the U.S. think that there is great animosity between the Tibetan and Chinese people. I have not found this to be true. To these Chinese students, the children at the special school were just kids who needed help.

Before they left for Lhasa, the students pulled an all-nighter to pack the books for the train ride. They bought their own train tickets for the 47-hour train trip from Beijing to Lhasa. They slept on the floor of the special school in sleeping bags for a month. They bought their own food for the trip. And they built a library, taught the children, cleared the school property and planted a garden so that the children would have fresh vegetables.

After a month of working together, the end of the trip was tough on everybody—it made the children cry when their new Chinese friends finally had to leave. After saying their many goodbyes to the children, the CAU students put on their backpacks and walked to the train station for the long ride home. I am sure this made Tara smile.

Fred and I are hoping to go to Tibet to visit the kids this summer, maybe with a box full of laptops. We are also working on a new project to help the kids in a school for migrant workers' children in Beijing, as well as another for grade school kids in North Korea.

## Preparing For a Career in Business

I have spoken to many groups of students in the U.S. and China. They all ask the same questions about how to be successful.

This is what I tell them. You can pass this on to the kids you know.

I tell them to worry less about what they do and more about what they are. Everyone with assets is searching for a person they can trust to manage them. In this, skills are good but principles are much more important. I suggested they read Stephen Covey's *First Things First*, which helps one understand the link between principles and objectives. I suggested they each prepare a personal mission statement and a statement of principles to use as a compass when making choices.

Beyond that, I strongly urged that they learn how to manage their time, the only resource they can truly control.

There aren't any secrets of success, but there are rules. Act in such a way that the people you want to learn from will want to have you around. Act in such a way that the people in charge will trust you to carry out any responsibilities they give you. Strive to become predictable in the same way that each can of Coca-Cola tastes exactly like the one before.

Many of the kids find my list of most important skills surprising.

At the top of the list—reading, writing and arithmetic, with basic accounting a close fourth. Read everything you can get your hands on—not just the things that confirm your opinions. Learn to read critically. Write lots of stuff every day. And don't dodge math courses. You will need those communications and math skills soon; you might as well learn them when you are in school.

Every college freshman should take two courses before the year begins: speed-reading and time management. Reading speed, more than anything else, determines how many ideas and points of view a student can absorb. I find it appalling that many people struggle along as slow readers when speed-reading is such an easy skill to learn.

As a high school student, I was fortunate to take a course that increased my reading speed to 2,700 words per minute. This has paid enormous dividends in my life. I still can't stand it that at my age there are so many things I have not yet read. But I'm gaining on them every night.

What about networking? Every opportunity in my career has been created by people who know and trust me, but making acquaintances so they can help you with your career is not the same thing. Don't network. Earn people's friendship.

What language would I study for the 21st century? I am a big fan of learning languages, both in and out of school, and have Italian, Russian, Arabic, Hindi and Chinese courses on my laptop. But if I could only study one language, I would learn Chinese. And I tell students in China to learn English (most of them already do). The U.S. and China are going to be the only two giants in the world economy in the future. We need to get to know each other.

When students ask me what to read during all the extra time they will gain by taking the speed-reading course, I talk to them about my favorite books. My list of favorites includes Gibbon's *The Decline & Fall of the Roman Empire*, Toynbee's *A Study of History*, Churchill's *A History of the English-Speaking Peoples*, Lyell's *Principles of Geology*, Boorstin's *The Discoverers* and *The Creators*, Feynman's *Six Easy Pieces*, Plutarch's *Parallel Lives*, Barabási's *Linked*, Wexler's *Brain and Culture*, Prigogine's *The End of Certainty*, Schneider and Sagan's *Into the Cool*, Schrödinger's *What is Life?*, Montague's *Why Choose This Book?*, Calvin's *The Cerebral Code*, Kandel's *In Search of Memory*, Hayek's *Individualism and Economic Order*, and (if you want to work really hard) Carver Mead's *Collective Electrodynamics*.

Recently, I received an e-mail from a young student that I had met while giving a lecture. After the lecture, he had bought a speed-reading course. His reading speed has doubled already. I love this job.

## Lessons from a Road Warrior

The best way to learn is to get out in the world, apply your energy and try a lot of stuff. Heck, some of it might even work! Here is the short list of lessons I learned along the way to becoming a better economist, a better investor and a better person:

1. Take care of your tools.

2. Don't bet against the second law of thermodynamics.

3. Watch for storms, but don't worry about getting wet once in a while.

4. Talk with the old guys. They have seen it before.

5. Figure out what you're good at—do that.

6. Figure out what you're not good at—stop doing that.

7. You don't have to raise your voice to be tough.

8. Travel a lot. Learn about other people.

9. Learn math.

10. Buy low—sell high. Carefully.

11. Stocks are always long-term investments.

12. Asset allocation is everything.

13. Jerks don't change.

14. If our brains were simple enough to understand, we would be too dumb to understand them.

15. Tara is watching.

# Bibliography

Acheson, D. J. (1990). *Elementary Fluid Dynamics*. Oxford, Oxford University Press.

Allais, M. (1947). *Economie et Intérêt: Présentation Nouvelle des Problèmes Fondamentaux Relatifs au Rôle Economique du Taux de l'Intérêt et de Leurs Solutions*. Paris, Librairie des Publications Officielles.

Asian Development Bank (2007). *Asian Development Outlook 2007*. Available at http://www.adb.org/Documents/Books/ADO/2007/default.asp.

Atkins, P. W. (1991). *Atoms, Electrons, and Change*. New York, Scientific American Library.

Atkins, P. W. (1994). *The Second Law*. New York, W.H. Freeman and Company.

Barabasi, A.-L. (2002). *Linked: How Everything is Connected to Everything Else and What it Means*. New York, Perseus Publishing.

Bartley, R. (1995). *The Seven Fat Years*. New York, Free Press.

Beinhocker, E. (2006). *The Origin of Wealth: Evolution, Complexity, and the Radical Remaking of Economics.* Boston, Harvard Business School Press.

Belshe, R. B. (2005). "The Origins of Pandemic Influenza: Lessons from the 1918 Virus." *The New England Journal of Medicine* 335(21): 2209-2211.

Bloom, H. K. (1997). *The Lucifer Principle: a Scientific expedition into the forces of history.* New York, Atlantic Monthly Press.

Boltzmann, L. (1886). "The Second Law of Thermodyamics." *Ludwig Boltzmann: Theoretical physics and philosophical problems: Selected writings.* B. Mcginnes. Dordrecht, Netherlands, D. Reidel, 1974.

Boorstin, D. (1983). *The Discoverers.* New York, Vintage.

Boorstin, D. (1993). *The Creators.* New York, Vintage.

Bramly, S. (1995). *Leonardo: the Artist and the Man.* New York, Penguin.

Buchanan, M. (2002). *Nexus: Small Worlds and the Groundbreaking Science of Networks* New York, W.W. Norton & Company.

Calvin, W. (1996). *The Cerebral Code: Thinking a Thought in the Mosaics of the Mind.* Cambridge, MA, MIT Press.

Canadian Copper and Brass Association (1997). "Laminar Flow and Turbulence." Available at http://www.coppercanada.ca/publications/is-97-02-publications-e.html.

Churchill, W. (1995). *History of the English-Speaking Peoples.* New York, Barnes & Noble.

Churchland, P. S. and T. J. Sejnowski (1992). *The Computational Brain.* Boston, MIT Press.

Covey, F., A. Merrill, et al. (1996). *First Things First.* New York, Free Press.

Davies, P. (2006). "Quantifying Energy." *BP Statistical Review of World Energy.* London, BP.

Dopfer (2005). *The Evolutionary Foundation of Economics.* London, Cambridge University Press.

Dressler, D. and H. Potter (1991). *Discovering Enzymes*. New York, W. H. Freeman and Company.

Drucker, P. (1946). *Concept of the Corporation*. New York, John Day Company.

Drucker, P. (1967). *The Effective Executive*. New York, HarperCollins.

Drucker, P. (1993). *Innovation and Entrepreneurship*. New York, Collins.

Einstein, A. (1905). "Does the Inertia of a Body Depend Upon Its Energy Content?" *Annalen der Physik*.

Energy Information Administration (2006). *Annual Energy Review 2005: Energy Perspectives*. Washington D.C., U.S. Government.

Federal Reserve (1978). *Balance Sheet of the United States*. Washington, DC, Board of Governors of the Federal Reserve System.

Federal Reserve (2007). *Flow of Funds Statement: Fourth Quarter*. Washington, DC, Board of Governors of the Federal Reserve System.

Feynman, R. P. (1989). *The Feynman Lectures on Physics*. Boston, Addison Wesley.

Feynman, R. P. (2005). *Six Easy Pieces: Essentials of Physics By Its Most Brilliant Teacher*. New York, Basic Books.

Friedman, H. (1986). *Sun and Earth*. New York, W.H. Freeman and Company.

Gibbon (1789). *The Decline & Fall of the Roman Empire*. London, Strahan & Cadell.

Gleick, J. (1987). *Chaos*. New York, Penguin Books.

Gordon, D. (2000). *Ants at Work: How an Insect Society is Organized*. New York, W. W. Norton & Company.

Graham, B. and D. Dodd (1934). *Security Analysis: Principles and Technique*. New York and London, McGraw-Hill Book Company, Inc.

Hamilton, B. A. (1978). *Study of World Economic Change*.

Hayek, F. A. (1948). *Individualism and Economic Order*. Chicago, University of Chicago Press.

Hayek, F. H. (1948). "Economics and Knowledge." *Individualism and Economic Order.* Chicago, University of Chicago Press: 33-56.

Hayek, F. H. (1948). "The Use of Knowledge in Society." *Individualism and Economic Order.* Chicago, University of Chicago Press: 77-91.

Hebb, D. O. (1949). *The Organization of Behavior,* Lawrence Erlbaum. 2002 ed.

Holland, J. (1995). *Hidden Order: How Adaption Builds Complexity.* Reading, MA, Helix Books.

Holldobler, B. and E. O. Wilson (1990). *The Ants.* New York, Belknap Press.

Jaffee, A. M. and M. E. Chen (2006). Testimony Before the US China Economic and Security Review Commission hearing on China's Role in the World.

Jaffee, A. M., M. E. Chen, et al. (2006). "China's Role in the World: Is China a Responsible Stakeholder?" *U.S.-China Economics and Security Review Commission.* Washington D.C. Available at http://www.uscc.gov/hearings/2006hearings/written_testimonies/06_08_3_4wrts/06_08_3_4_jaffee_amy_statement.pdf

Johnson, R. (1998). *The Handbook of Fluid Dynamics.* New York, CRC.

Kahneman, D., P. Slovik, et al. (1982). *Judgment Under Uncertainty: Heuristics and Biases.* Cambridge, Cambridge University Press.

Kandel, E., J. H. Schwartz, et al., Eds. (2000). *Principles of Neural Science.* New York, McGraw Hill.

Kandel, E. R. (2006). *In Search of Memory.* New York, W. W. Norton & Company.

Kauffman, S. (1993). *The Origins of Order.* New York, Oxford University Press, USA.

Keynes, J. M. (1936). *The General Theory of Employment, Interest and Money.* London, Macmillan.

Kondepudi, D. and I. Prigogine (1998). *Modern Thermodynamics: From Heat Engines to Dissipative Structures.* New York, John Wiley & Sons.

Lee, A. (1989). *Call Me Roger.* Chicago, McGraw-Hill Contemporary.

Locke, J. (1690). *An Essay Concerning Human Understanding.* London.

Lotka, A. J. (1956). *Elements of Mathematical Biology.* New York, Dover Publications.

Lotka, A. J. (2006) *Analytical Theory and Biological Populations.* New York, Springer.

Lyell, C. and J. A. Secord (1998). *Principles of Geology.* New York, Penguin Classics.

Machievelli, N. (1515). *The Prince.*

Maiklem, L., ed. (1998). *Ultimate Visual Dictionary of Science.* New York, DK Publishing.

Marshall, A. (1890). *Principles of Economics.* London, Macmillan and Co, Ltd.

Mead, C. A. (2000). *Collective Electrodynamics: Quantum Foundations of Electromagnetism.* Cambridge, MA, MIT Publishing.

Mises, L. von (1949). *Human Action: a Treatise on Economics.* Hartford, CT, Yale University Press.

Montague, R. (2006). *Why Choose This Book?* New York, Dutton Adult.

Nicolis, G. and I. Prigogine (1989). *Exploring Complexity: An Introduction* New York, W.H. Freeman & Company.

Odum, H. T. (1971). *Environment, Power, and Society.* New York, John Wiley & Sons Inc.

Peterson, R. (2007). *Inside the Investor's Brain.* New York, Wiley.

Plutarch (2001). *Plutarch's Lives.* New York, Modern Library.

Prigogine, I. (1997). *The End of Certainty.* New York, The Free Press.

Ricardo, D. (1817). *On the Principles of Political Economy and Taxation.* London, G. Bell & Sons.

Rutledge, J. (1973). *A Monetarist Model of Inflationary Expectations.* Lexington, MA, Lexington Books.

Rutledge, J. (1981). "Why Interest Rates Will Fall in 1982." *Wall Street Journal*. New York.

Rutledge, J. (2007). "Energy Model of Economic Activity." Newport Beach, CA.

Rutledge, J. (2007). "Asia's Energy Security and the Middle East." *BOAO Forum*. Boao, China.

Rutledge, J. and D. Allen (1989). *Rust to Riches*. New York, Harper & Row.

Schneider, E. D. and D. Sagan (2005). *Into the Cool: Energy Flow, Thermodynamics, and Life*. Chicago, University of Chicago Press.

Schrödinger, I. (1944). *What Is Life?* London, Cambridge University Press.

Schumpeter, J. A. (2005). "Development." *Journal of Economic Literature* 43(1): 108-120.

Singer, S. F. and D. T. Avery (2007). *Unstoppable Global Warming: Every 1500 Years*. London, Rowman and Littlefield Publishers.

Sloan, A. (1964). *My Years with General Motors*. New York, Doubleday.

Stigler, G. (1946). *The Theory of Price*. New York, MacMillan.

Strogatz, S. (2003). *Sync: The Emerging Science of Spontaneous Order*. New York, Hyperion.

Taubenberger, J., A. Reid, et al. (2005). "Characterization of the 1918 influenza virus polymerase genes." *Nature* 437: 889-893.

Toynbee, A. J. (1987). *A Study of History*. London, Oxford University Press.

Tumpey, T., C. Basler, et al. (2005). "Characterization of the reconstructed 1918 Spanish influenza pandemic virus." *Science* 310: 77-80.

Turing, A. M. (1952). "The Chemical Basis of Morphogenesis." *Philosophical Transactions of the Royal Society of London. Series B, Biological Sciences* 237(641): 37-72.

van Dyke, M. (1982). *An Album of Fluid Motion*. Stanford, CA, Parabolic Press.

Watts, D. J. (2002). "A simple model of global cascades on random networks." *Proceedings of the National Academy of Sciences* 99(9): 5,766–5,771.

Watts, D. J. (2003). *Small Worlds: The Dynamics of Networks between Order and Randomness* Princeton, NJ, Princeton University Press.

Watts, D. J. (2003). *Six Degrees: The Science of a Connected Age*. New York, W.W. Norton & Company.

Wexler, B. E. (2006). *Brain and Culture: Neurobiology, Ideology, and Social Change*. Cambridge, MA, The MIT Press.

Wilson, E. O. (1975). *Sociobiology*. New York, Belknap Press.

# Index

2947222

Made in the USA